JavaMail API

Elliotte Rusty Harold

O'REILLY®

Beijing · Cambridge · Farnham · Köln · Sebastopol · Tokyo

JavaMail API

by Elliotte Rusty Harold

Printed in the United States of America.

Published by O'Reilly Media, Inc., 1005 Gravenstein Highway North, Sebastopol, CA 95472.

O'Reilly books may be purchased for educational, business, or sales promotional use. Online editions are also available for most titles (*http://my.safaribooksonline.com*). For more information, contact our corporate/institutional sales department: 800-998-9938 or *corporate@oreilly.com*.

Editor: Meghan Blanchette
Production Editor: Melanie Yarbrough
Proofreader: Nicole Shelby

Cover Designer: Randy Comer
Interior Designer: David Futato
Illustrator: Rebecca Demarest

July 2013:   First Edition

Revision History for the First Edition:

2013-07-22:   First release

See *http://oreilly.com/catalog/errata.csp?isbn=9781449367244* for release details.

ISBN: 978-1-449-36724-4

[LSI]

Table of Contents

Preface

Email was the Internet's first killer app. One of the most frequently asked questions about Java is how to send email from a Java applet or application. While it's certainly possible to write a Java program that uses sockets to communicate with mail servers, this requires detailed knowledge of some fairly complicated protocols, such as SMTP, POP, and IMAP. Just as the URL class makes interacting with HTTP servers a lot simpler than it would be with raw sockets, so too can a class library dedicated to handling email make writing email clients a lot simpler.

The JavaMail API is a standard extension to Java that provides a class library for email clients. It's a required component of the Java Platform, Enterprise Edition. The JavaMail API can be implemented in pure Java using sockets and streams, and indeed Oracle's reference implementation is so implemented. Programs use the JavaMail API to communicate with SMTP, POP, and IMAP servers to send and receive email. By taking advantage of this API, you can avoid focusing on the low-level protocol details and focus instead on what you want to say with the message. Custom providers can support the proprietary features of mail systems such as Gmail and Microsoft Exchange. You can even install providers that add support for NNTP, the protocol used to transport Usenet news.

There's no limit to the uses Java programs have for the JavaMail API. Most obviously, you can write standard email clients such as Thunderbird. Or it can be used for email-intensive applications such as mailing list managers, like listproc. But the JavaMail API is also useful as a part of larger applications that simply need to send or receive a little email. For instance, a server-monitoring application can periodically load pages from a web server running on a different host and email the webmaster if the web server has crashed. An applet can use email to send data to any process or person on the Internet that has an email address, in essence using the web server's SMTP server as a simple proxy to bypass the usual security restrictions about whom an applet is allowed to talk to. In reverse, an applet can talk to an IMAP server on the applet host to receive data from many hosts around the Net. A newsreader could be implemented as a custom service provider that treats NNTP as just one more means of exchanging messages. And that's just the beginning of the sort of programs the JavaMail API makes it very straight-forward to write.

Who You Are

This book assumes you are comfortable with the Java language and programming environment, in addition to object-oriented programming in general. This book does not attempt to be a basic language tutorial. You should be thoroughly familiar with the syntax of Java. You should have written at least simple applications.

Java Versions

This book is written with the assumption that you are coding with at least Java 5.0. In general, I use Java 5 features like generics and the enhanced for loop freely without further explanation. With respect to the JavaMail API, the distinction between Java 5 and Java 6 is not large. Most examples look identical in the two versions.

Java 7 is a bit more of a stretch. I have not shied away from using features introduced in Java 7 where they seemed especially useful or convenient—for instance, try-with-resources and multicatch are both very helpful when fitting examples into the limited space available in a printed book—but I have been careful to point out my use of such features.

As to JavaMail itself, this book covers JavaMail 1.5 which requires Java 5 or later. If for some reason you're stuck on Java 1.4, JavaMail 1.4.1 is still available and will work with your JDK. Whichever version you use, the JavaMail API is not bundled with the base JDK or JRE, even in Java 8. You can download it separately from *https://java.net/projects/javamail/*.

Conventions Used in This Book

Body text is Times Roman, normal, like you're reading now.

A `monospaced typewriter font` is used for:

- Code examples and fragments
- Anything that might appear in a Java program, including keywords, operators, data types, method names, variable names, class names, and interface names
- Program output
- Tags that might appear in an HTML document

A **`bold monospaced font`** is used for:

- Command lines and options that should be typed verbatim on the screen

An *italicized* font is used for:

- New terms where they are defined
- Pathnames, filenames, and program names (however, if the program name is also the name of a Java class, it is given in a monospaced font, like other class names)
- Host and domain names (*java.oreilly.com*)
- URLs (*http://www.cafeaulait.org/slides/*)
- Titles of other chapters and books (*Java I/O*)

Significant code fragments and complete programs are generally placed into a separate paragraph, like this:

```
Message msg = new MimeMessage(session);
Address elliotte = new InternetAddress("elharo@ibiblio.org");
msg.setFrom(elliotte);
```

When code is presented as fragments rather than complete programs, the existence of the appropriate `import` statements should be inferred. For example, in the above code fragment you may assume that `javax.mail.Address` and `javax.mail.Message` were imported.

 Indicates a tip, suggestion, or general note.

 Indicates a warning or caution.

Request for Comments

I enjoy hearing from readers, whether with general comments about this book, specific corrections, other topics you would like to see covered, or just war stories about your own network programming travails. You can reach me by sending email to *elharo@ibi blio.org*. Please realize, however, that I receive several hundred pieces of email a day and cannot personally respond to each one. For the best chances of getting a personal response, please identify yourself as a reader of this book. If you have a question about a particular program that isn't working as you expect, try to reduce it to the simplest case that reproduces the bug, preferably a single class, and paste the text of the entire program into the *body* of your email. Unsolicited attachments will be deleted unopened. And please, please send the message from the account you want me to reply to and make sure that your Reply-to address is properly set! There's nothing quite so frustrating as spending an hour or more carefully researching the answer to an interesting question and composing a detailed response, only to have it bounce because my correspondent was sending from a public terminal and neglected to set the browser preferences to include their actual email address.

I also adhere to the old saying "If you like this book, tell your friends. If you don't like it, tell me." I'm especially interested in hearing about mistakes. This is my eighth book. I've yet to publish a perfect one, but I keep trying. As hard as I and the editors at O'Reilly worked on this book, I'm sure there are mistakes and typographical errors that we missed here somewhere. And I'm sure that at least one of them is a really embarrassing whopper of a problem. If you find a mistake or a typo, please let me know so I can correct it. I'll post it on the O'Reilly website (*http://www.oreilly.com/catalog/javamail/errata/*). Before reporting errors, please check one of those pages to see if I already know about it and have posted a fix. Any errors that are reported will be fixed in future printings.

Using Code Examples

This book is here to help you get your job done. In general, if this book includes code examples, you may use the code in this book in your programs and documentation. You do not need to contact us for permission unless you're reproducing a significant portion of the code. For example, writing a program that uses several chunks of code from this book does not require permission. Selling or distributing a CD-ROM of examples from O'Reilly books does require permission. Answering a question by citing this book and quoting example code does not require permission. Incorporating a significant amount of example code from this book into your product's documentation does require permission.

We appreciate, but do not require, attribution. An attribution usually includes the title, author, publisher, and ISBN. For example: "*JavaMail API* by Elliotte Rusty Harold (O'Reilly). Copyright 2013 Elliotte Rusty Harold, 978-1-449-36724-4."

If you feel your use of code examples falls outside fair use or the permission given above, feel free to contact us at *permissions@oreilly.com*.

Safari® Books Online

 *Safari Books Online* is an on-demand digital library that delivers expert content in both book and video form from the world's leading authors in technology and business.

Technology professionals, software developers, web designers, and business and creative professionals use Safari Books Online as their primary resource for research, problem solving, learning, and certification training.

Safari Books Online offers a range of product mixes and pricing programs for organizations, government agencies, and individuals. Subscribers have access to thousands of books, training videos, and prepublication manuscripts in one fully searchable database from publishers like O'Reilly Media, Prentice Hall Professional, Addison-Wesley Professional, Microsoft Press, Sams, Que, Peachpit Press, Focal Press, Cisco Press, John Wiley & Sons, Syngress, Morgan Kaufmann, IBM Redbooks, Packt, Adobe Press, FT Press, Apress, Manning, New Riders, McGraw-Hill, Jones & Bartlett, Course Technology, and dozens more. For more information about Safari Books Online, please visit us online.

How to Contact Us

Please address comments and questions concerning this book to the publisher:

O'Reilly Media, Inc.
1005 Gravenstein Highway North
Sebastopol, CA 95472
800-998-9938 (in the United States or Canada)
707-829-0515 (international or local)
707-829-0104 (fax)

We have a web page for this book, where we list errata, examples, and any additional information. You can access this page at *http://oreil.ly/javamail-api*.

To comment or ask technical questions about this book, send email to *bookquestions@oreilly.com*.

For more information about our books, courses, conferences, and news, see our website at *http://www.oreilly.com*.

Find us on Facebook: *http://facebook.com/oreilly*

Follow us on Twitter: *http://twitter.com/oreillymedia*

Watch us on YouTube: *http://www.youtube.com/oreillymedia*

Acknowledgments

Many people were involved in the production of this book.

Edward Wong, Alex Stangl, and Bill Shannon ably reviewed early drafts and substantially improved the coverage of many topics. Development editor Meghan Blanchette shepherded the book through the contract, writing, editing, and production process with grace and aplomb. It isn't customary to thank the publisher, but the publisher does set the tone for the rest of the company, authors, editors, and production staff alike; and I think Tim O'Reilly deserves special credit for making O'Reilly Media absolutely one of the best houses an author can write for. If there's one person without whom this book would never have been written, it's him. If you, the reader, find O'Reilly books to be consistently better than most of the drek on the market, the reason really can be traced straight back to Tim.

Finally, as always, I'd like to offer my largest thanks for my wife, Beth, without whose love and support this book would never have happened.

—Elliotte Rusty Harold
elharo@ibiblio.org
June 19, 2013

CHAPTER 1

Introducing the JavaMail API

The JavaMail API is a fairly high-level representation of the basic components of any email system. The components are represented by abstract classes in the `javax.mail` package. For instance, the abstract class `javax.mail.Message` represents an email message. It declares abstract methods to get and set various kinds of envelope information for the message, such as the sender and addressee, the date sent, and the subject. The abstract class `javax.mail.Folder` represents a message container. It declares abstract methods to retrieve messages from a folder, move messages between folders, and delete messages from a folder.

These classes are all abstract because they don't make many assumptions about how the email is stored or transferred between machines. For instance, they do not assume that messages are sent using SMTP or that they're structured as specified in RFC 822. Concrete subclasses of these classes specialize the abstract classes to particular protocols and mail formats. If you want to work with standard Internet email, you might use `javax.mail.MimeMessage` instead of `javax.mail.Message`, `javax.mail.InternetAddress` instead of `javax.mail.Address`, and `com.sun.mail.imap.IMAPStore` instead of `javax.mail.Store`. If you were writing code for a Microsoft Exchange-based system, you'd use different concrete implementation classes but the same abstract base classes.

The JavaMail API roughly follows the abstract factory design pattern. This pattern allows you to write your code based on the abstract superclasses without worrying too much about the lower-level details. The protocols and formats used and the associated concrete implementation classes are determined mostly by one line of code early in the program that names the protocol. Changing the protocol name goes 90% of the way toward porting your program from one protocol (say, POP) to another (say, IMAP).

Service providers implement particular protocols. A service provider is a group of concrete subclasses of the abstract JavaMail API classes that specialize the general API to a particular protocol and mail format. These subclasses are probably (though not necessarily) organized into one package. Some of these (IMAP, SMTP) are provided with the reference implementation in the undocumented com.sun.mail package. Others (NNTP, Exchange) are available from third parties. And some (POP) are available from both Oracle and third parties. The purpose of the abstract JavaMail API is to shield you from low-level details like this. You don't write code to access an IMAP server or a POP server; you write code that speaks to the JavaMail API. Then the JavaMail API uses the service provider to speak to the server using its native protocol. This is middleware for email. All you need to do to add a new protocol is install the service provider's JAR file. Simple, carefully designed programs that use only the core features of the JavaMail API may be able to use the new provider without even being recompiled. Of course, programs that make use of special features of individual protocols may need to be rewritten.

Since mail arrives from the network at unpredictable times, the JavaMail API relies on an event-based callback mechanism to handle incoming mail. This is exactly the same pattern (even using some of the same classes) found in the Swing and JavaBeans. The javax.mail.event package defines about half a dozen different kinds of mail events, as well as the associated listener interfaces and adapter classes for these events.

While many people still fondly recall the early days of ASCII email and even ASCII pictures, modern email messages contain a bewildering array of multilingual text and multimedia data encoded in formats such as Base64, quoted-printable, BinHex, and uuencode. To handle this, the JavaMail API uses the JavaBeans Activation Framework (JAF) to describe and display this content.

This book covers Version 1.5 of the JavaMail API. The JavaMail API is a standard extension to Java, not part of the core JDK or JRE class library, even in Java 8. (It is a standard part of Java Enterprise Edition (JEE)). Consequently, you'll need to download it separately from Oracle and install it on your system. It's freely available from Java (*https://java.net/projects/javamail/$$*). It comes as a JAR archive named *javax.mail.jar*. This file contains the actual *.class* files that implement the JavaMail API. To compile or run the examples in this book, you'll need to add this file to your class path, either by adding its path to the CLASSPATH environment variable or by placing *javax.mail.jar* in your *jre/lib/ext* directory.

If you're using Java 5, you will also need to install the JavaBeans Activation Framework. (It's bundled with the JDK starting in Java 6.) You can download it from Oracle's website (*http://www.oracle.com/technetwork/java/javase/index-jsp-136939.html$$*). This download contains the *activation.jar* archive, which you'll also need to place in your class path.

Finally, you may want to add some additional providers. Oracle's implementation includes POP3, SMTP, Gmail, and IMAP providers. However, third parties have written providers for other protocols such as Hotmail, NNTP, Exchange, and more. Table 1-1 lists some of these.

Table 1-1. Mail providers

Product (company)	URL	Protocols	License
JavaMail (Oracle)	http://www.oracle.com/technetwork/java/java mail	SMTP, IMAP, POP3, Gmail	GPL with Classpath Exception
J-Integra Exchange: (Intrinsyc Software)	http://j-integra.intrinsyc.com/exchange.asp	Microsoft Exchange (DCOM)	Payware
exJello: (Eric Glass)	http://www.exjello.org/	Microsoft Exchange (WebDAV)	MIT License
ICE MH JavaMail Provider (ICE Engineering, Inc.)	http://www.trustice.com/java/icemh	MH	Public domain
POPpers (Y. Miyadate)	http://www2s.biglobe.ne.jp/~dat/java/project/ poppers/index_en.html	POP3	GPL
JDAVMail (Luc Claes)	http://jdavmail.sourceforge.net	Hotmail (WebDAV)	LGPL
GNU JavaMail (FSF)	http://www.gnu.org/software/classpathx/java mail/	POP3, NNTP, SMTP, IMAP, mbox, maildir	GPL with library exception
mbox Store (Oracle)	https://java.net/projects/javamail/pages/Mbox Store	mbox	

CHAPTER 2

Sending Email

Sending messages is the most basic email need of a Java program. While email clients like Thunderbird and mailing list managers like listproc are the only common programs that receive messages, all sorts of programs send messages. For instance, web browsers can submit HTML forms via email. Security scanning tools can run in the background and email their results to the administrator when they're done. When the Unix cron program detects a misconfigured *crontab* file, it emails the error to the owner. Books & Writers runs a popular service that tracks the sales rank of authors' books on Amazon.com and notifies them periodically via email. A massively parallel computation like the *SETI@home* project can submit individual results via email. Some multiplayer games like chess can be played across the network by emailing the moves back and forth (though this scheme wouldn't work for speed chess). And these are just a few of the different kinds of programs that send email. In today's wired world, by far the simplest way to notify users of an event when they're not sitting in front of the computer that the program is running on is to send them an email.

The JavaMail API provides everything programs need to send email. To send a message, a program follows these steps:

1. Place properties for the session in a `Properties` object.

2. Start a mail session with the `Session.getInstance()` method.

3. Create a new `Message` object, probably by instantiating one of its concrete subclasses.

4. Set the message's From: address.

5. Set the message's To: address.

6. Set the message's Subject:.

7. Set the content of the message.

8. Get a `Transport` from the session.

9. Connect the transport to a named host using a username and password.

10. Send the message to all recipients over the transport.

Individually, each of the steps is quite simple.

The first step is to start a `Session` with a specified group of properties using the `Session.getInstance()` factory method, like this:

```
Properties props = new Properties();
Session session = Session.getInstance(props);
```

For the moment, we'll just accept the default properties. For future reference, Table 2-1 lists the most common system properties that control sending messages. Note the general pattern that `mail.foo` sets the foo property for all protocols (SMTP, NNTP, IMAP, etc.) while `mail.protocol_name.foo` overrides the foo property for the named protocol. For instance, if `mail.host` is set to *mail.example.com* and `mail.smtp.host` is set to *smtp.gmail.com* then IMAP and POP will retrieve messages from *mail.example.com* but SMTP will send via *smtp.gmail.com*. In most cases, the default values provided by system properties can be overridden when invoking a particular method.

Table 2-1. System properties used for sending mail

Property	Default Value	Purpose
mail.host		Host name of the mail server
mail.smtp.host		Host name of the SMTP server; overrides mail.host for SMTP connections only
mail.*protocol*.host		Host name of the server for the specified protocol. Overrides mail.host
mail.user		Default username sent to mail servers
mail.*protocol*.user		Default username sent to servers for the specified protocol; e.g., mail.smtp.user for an SMTP server or mail.smtps.user for an SMTPS server; overrides mail.user
mail.smtp.port	25	Port on which the SMTP server is listening
mail.*protocol*.port	default port for the protocol	Port on which the server for the specified protocol is listening
mail.smtp.starttls.enable		Upgrade the regular SMTP connection on the usual port to an encrypted (TLS or SSL) connection
mail.smtp.connectiontimeout	infinite	Number of milliseconds to wait for a connection before hanging up
mail.debug	false	Print various debugging information to the console
mail.from		The email address to use in the From: header
mail.mime.charset	file.encoding	Default character set used to send messages. You should always set this to UTF-8
mail.transport.protocol.*address-type*		The message transport protocol such as SMTP for the specified address type; e.g., mail.transport.protocol.rfc822

Property	Default Value	Purpose
mail.*protocol*.class		Fully package qualified class name of the provider for the specified protocol
mail.transport.protocol	first transport provider in the configuration file	Default protocol with which to send messages
mail.alternates		Other email addresses for the current user that will not be included when replying to a message
mail.replyallcc	false	When replying to all, put all recipients in the Cc list of the reply message instead of the To field

This `Session` object is then used to construct a new `Message` object:

```
Message msg = new MimeMessage(session);
```

Here I specify the `MimeMessage` class in particular since I know I'm sending Internet email. However, this is the one place where I do explicitly choose a format for the email message.

Now that I have a `Message` object, I need to set up its fields and contents. The From: address and To: address will each be `javax.mail.internet.InternetAddress` objects. You can provide either an email address alone or an email address and a personal name:

```
Address bill = new InternetAddress("god@microsoft.com", "Bill Gates");
Address elliotte = new InternetAddress("elharo@ibiblio.org");
```

The `setFrom()` method specifies who's sending the message by setting the From: header. There's no protection against forgery. It's quite easy for me to masquerade as Bill Gates at a (presumably) fictitious email address:

```
msg.setFrom(bill);
```

The `setRecipient()` method is slightly more complex. You not only have to specify the address that the message will be sent to, but how that address is used; that is, as a To: field, a Cc: field, or a Bcc: field. These are indicated by three mnemonic constants of the `Message.RecipientType` class:

```
Message.RecipientType.TO
Message.RecipientType.CC
Message.RecipientType.BCC
```

For example:

```
msg.setRecipient(Message.RecipientType.TO, elliotte);
```

The subject is set as a simple string of text. For example:

```
msg.setSubject("You must comply.");
```

The body is also set as a single string of text. For example:

```
msg.setText("Resistance is futile. You will be assimilated!");
```

Next we specify the transport we want. In 2013, smtps (SMTP over TLS) is the customary choice:

```
Transport t = session.getTransport("smtps");
```

Once you have a transport, you connect it to a specified host with a given username and password:

```
t.connect("smtp.gmail.com", "elharo", "mypassword");
```

 SMTP connections used to be unauthenticated with no username or password. However, spammer abuse made this sort of open relay infeasible in the 21st century. Going forward, even usernames and passwords are less than perfectly secure. I would not be surprised if this example stops working during the lifetime of this book and some more secure oAuth2 or two factor system becomes required to send email.

Next the send() method connects to the mail server and sends the message on its way:

```
t.sendMessage(msg, msg.getAllRecipients());
```

The second argument to sendMessage() is an array of addresses to send the message to. Instead of using the addresses in the message itself, you could add additional email addresses. For example:

```
Address[] addresses = {
  new InternetAddress("wilma@example.org"),
  new InternetAddress("fred@example.org"),
  new InternetAddress("daphne@example.org"),
  new InternetAddress("shaggy@example.org")
};

transport.sendMessage(msg, addresses);
```

Finally the close() method shuts down the connection. Transport does not implement AutoCloseable, so even in Java 7 programs normally use the dispose pattern and close the transport in a finally block:

```
Transport t;
try {
  // work with the transport...
} catch (MessagingException ex) {
  ex.printStackTrace();
} finally {
  if (t != null) {
    try {
      t.close();
    } catch (MessagingException ex) {
```

```
      }
    }
  }
```

You can actually bundle almost all these steps up into a single static method call:

```
Transport.send(msg, "username", "password");
```

If you do this, the SMTP server is read from the system property mail.smtp.host.

Example 2-1 puts all these steps together into a standalone program that sends the following message:

```
Date: Fri, 29 Nov 2013 15:55:42 -0500 (EST)
From: Bill Gates <god@microsoft.com>
To: elharo@ibiblio.org
Subject: You must comply.

Resistance is futile. You will be assimilated!
```

I've shown this message in standard RFC 822 format used for Internet email. However, that isn't necessary. You just need to know the recipient (*elharo@ibiblio.org*), the sender (*god@microsoft.com*), and the subject and body of the message. The JavaMail API handles details of the underlying protocol.

Example 2-1. Sending a very simple mail message

```
import javax.mail.*;
import javax.mail.internet.*;

import java.io.UnsupportedEncodingException;
import java.util.*;

public class Assimilator {

  public static void main(String[] args) {
    Properties props = new Properties();
    Session session = Session.getInstance(props);
    MimeMessage msg = new MimeMessage(session);

    Transport t = null;
    try {
      Address bill = new InternetAddress("god@microsoft.com", "Bill Gates");
      Address elliotte = new InternetAddress("elharo@ibiblio.org");

      msg.setText("Resistance is futile. You will be assimilated!");
      msg.setFrom(bill);
      msg.setRecipient(Message.RecipientType.TO, elliotte);
      msg.setSubject("You must comply.");

      t = session.getTransport("smtps");
      t.connect("smtp.gmail.com", "erharold", "password");
      t.sendMessage(msg, msg.getAllRecipients());
    } catch (MessagingException | UnsupportedEncodingException ex) {
```

```
      ex.printStackTrace();
    } finally { // Transport does not implement AutoCloseable :-(
      if (t != null) {
        try {
          t.close();
        } catch (MessagingException ex) {
        }
      }
    }
  }
}
```

In this example I've taken advantage of multi-catch from Java 7. Unfortunately Trans
port does not implement AutoCloseable—the JavaMail API still needs to be compatible
with Java 6—so I do have to check whether the transport object is non-null, close it,
and catch and ignore any exceptions while closing, all in a finally block.

An alternative is to use the static Transport.send() method introduced in JavaMail
1.5, which does close itself internally. To do this, you configure the connection with
system properties.

```
Properties props = new Properties();
props.put("mail.smtp.host", "smtp.gmail.com");
props.put("mail.transport.protocol", "smtps");
Session session = Session.getInstance(props);
MimeMessage msg = new MimeMessage(session);

try {
  Address bill = new InternetAddress("god@microsoft.com",  "Bill Gates");
  Address elliotte = new InternetAddress("elharo@ibiblio.org");

  msg.setText("Resistance is futile. You will be assimilated!");
  msg.setFrom(bill);
  msg.setRecipient(Message.RecipientType.TO, elliotte);
  msg.setSubject("You must comply.");

  Transport.send(msg, "erharold", "password");
} catch (MessagingException | UnsupportedEncodingException ex) {
  ex.printStackTrace();
}
```

Sending Email from an Application

Example 2-1 is a simple application that sends a fixed message to a known address with
a specified subject. Once you see how to do this, it's straightforward to replace the strings
that give the message address, subject, and body with data read from the command line,
a GUI, a database, or some other source. For instance, Example 2-2 is a very simple GUI
for sending email. Figure 2-1 shows the program running.

Figure 2-1. A simple GUI mail program

The mail code is all tied up in the `actionPerformed()` method and looks very similar to the `main()` method of Example 2-1. It is activated when the user presses the "Send Message" button. The big difference is that now the host, username, password, subject, From: address, To: address, and text of the message are all read from the GUI components at runtime rather than being hardcoded as string literals in the source code. The rest of the code is related to setting up the GUI and has little to do with the JavaMail API.

Example 2-2. A graphical SMTP client

```
import javax.mail.*;
import javax.mail.internet.*;
import java.util.*;
import javax.swing.*;
```

```
import java.awt.event.*;
import java.awt.*;

public class SMTPClient extends JFrame {

  private JTextField   fromField       = new JTextField(40);
  private JTextField   toField         = new JTextField(40);
  private JTextField   hostField       = new JTextField(40);
  private JTextField   subjectField    = new JTextField(40);
  private JTextField   usernameField   = new JTextField(40);
  private JTextField   passwordField   = new JPasswordField(40);
  private JTextArea    message         = new JTextArea(40, 72);
  private JScrollPane  jsp             = new JScrollPane(message);

  public SMTPClient() {
    super("SMTP Client");

    Container contentPane = this.getContentPane();
    contentPane.setLayout(new BorderLayout());

    JPanel labels = new JPanel();
    labels.setLayout(new GridLayout(6, 1));

    JLabel hostLabel = new JLabel("SMTP Server: ");
    labels.add(hostLabel);

    JPanel fields = new JPanel();
    fields.setLayout(new GridLayout(6, 1));
    String host = System.getProperty("mail.host", "smtp.gmail.com");
    hostField.setText(host);
    fields.add(hostField);

    JLabel toLabel = new JLabel("To: ");
    labels.add(toLabel);
    fields.add(toField);

    String from = System.getProperty("mail.from", "");
    fromField.setText(from);
    JLabel fromLabel = new JLabel("From: ");
    labels.add(fromLabel);
    fields.add(fromField);

    JLabel subjectLabel = new JLabel("Subject: ");
    labels.add(subjectLabel);
    fields.add(subjectField);

    JLabel usernameLabel = new JLabel("Username: ");
    labels.add(usernameLabel);
    fields.add(usernameField);

    JLabel passwordLabel = new JLabel("Password: ");
```

```java
      labels.add(passwordLabel);
      fields.add(passwordField);

      Box north = Box.createHorizontalBox();
      north.add(Box.createHorizontalStrut(5));
      north.add(labels);
      north.add(fields);

      contentPane.add(north, BorderLayout.NORTH);

      message.setFont(new Font("Monospaced", Font.PLAIN, 12));
      contentPane.add(jsp, BorderLayout.CENTER);

      JPanel south = new JPanel();
      south.setLayout(new FlowLayout(FlowLayout.CENTER));
      JButton sendButton = new JButton("Send Message");
      south.add(sendButton);
      sendButton.addActionListener(new SendAction());
      contentPane.add(south, BorderLayout.SOUTH);

      this.pack();
   }

   private class SendAction implements ActionListener {

      @Override
      public void actionPerformed(ActionEvent evt) {
         try {
            Properties props = new Properties();
            final Session session = Session.getInstance(props);
            final Message msg = new MimeMessage(session);

            Address to = new InternetAddress(toField.getText());
            Address from = new InternetAddress(fromField.getText());

            msg.setContent(message.getText(), "text/plain");
            msg.setFrom(from);
            msg.setRecipient(Message.RecipientType.TO, to);
            msg.setSubject(subjectField.getText());

            final String hostname = hostField.getText();
            final String username = usernameField.getText();
            final String password = passwordField.getText();

            // Sending a message can take a non-trivial amount of time so
            // spawn a thread to handle it.
            Runnable r = new Runnable() {
               @Override
               public void run() {
                  Transport t = null;
                  try {
                     t = session.getTransport("smtps");
```

```
                t.connect(hostname, username, password);
                t.sendMessage(msg, msg.getAllRecipients());
              } catch (MessagingException ex) {
                ex.printStackTrace();
              } finally { // Transport does not implement Autocloseable :-(
                if (t != null)
                  try {
                    t.close();
                  } catch (MessagingException e) {
                    // ignore
                  }
              }
            }
          }
        };
        Thread t = new Thread(r);
        t.start();

        message.setText("");
      } catch (MessagingException ex) {
        JOptionPane.showMessageDialog(getRootPane(),
            "Error sending message: " + ex.getMessage());
      }
    }
  }

  public static void main(String[] args) {

    SwingUtilities.invokeLater(new Runnable() {
      @Override
      public void run() {
        SMTPClient client = new SMTPClient();
        // I set up the exit behavior here rather than in
        // the constructor since other programs that use this class
        // may not want to exit the application when the SMTPClient
        // window closes.
        client.setDefaultCloseOperation(JFrame.EXIT_ON_CLOSE);
        client.setVisible(true);
      }
    });
  }
}
```

This is far from an ideal program. The GUI could be more cleanly separated from the mailing code. And it would be better to bring up an error dialog if something went wrong rather than just printing a stack trace of the exception on System.err. However, since none of that would teach us anything about the JavaMail API, I leave it all as an exercise for the interested reader.

CHAPTER 3

Receiving Mail

Receiving mail is considerably more complex than sending it. SMTP uses only 14 different commands, and a simple email client can be implemented with just five of them. POP3, however, has 12 commands, almost all of which a client must be able to handle; IMAP4 has 24 different commands.

The JavaMail API is designed to retrieve messages from an IMAP or perhaps an NNTP server. That is, it assumes the server can return headers separate from the messages they belong to, search through mailboxes, provide the storage for the messages rather than the client, and so forth. The JavaMail API provides less of what you need for client-oriented mail access protocols, such as POP3, that assume the client stores and manages the mail archive; but it still gives you the tools you need to download the mail from the server. You just have to implement your own storage system on the client. (You can check out the experimental POP3RemoteStore (*https://java.net/projects/javamail/pages/POP3RemoteStore*) if you want to both store and retrieve.)

We'll begin with the simpler POP3 protocol, then move on to IMAP. From the perspective of JavaMail, IMAP can be viewed largely as POP plus some commands for manipulating folders. For simple programs that operate only on the INBOX folder, POP and IMAP clients are more or less the same.

There are about 12 steps to reading a remote mailbox (the number of steps can vary a little, since some steps are optional or can be combined with or replaced by others):

1. Set up the properties you'll use for the connection.

2. Construct the `Authenticator` you'll use for the connection.

3. Get a `Session` object with `Session.getInstance()`.

4. Use the session's `getStore()` method to return a `Store`.

5. Connect to the store.

6. Get the INBOX folder from the store with the `getFolder()` method.

7. Open the INBOX folder.

8. Open the folder you want inside the INBOX folder. Repeat as many times as necessary to reach the folder you're seeking.

9. Get the messages from the folder as an array of `Message` objects.

10. Iterate through the array of messages, processing each one in turn using the methods of the `Message` class. For instance, you might print out each message or simply display the sender, subject, and other vital information in a GUI for the user to select from, as in Figure 3-1.

11. Close the folder.

12. Close the store.

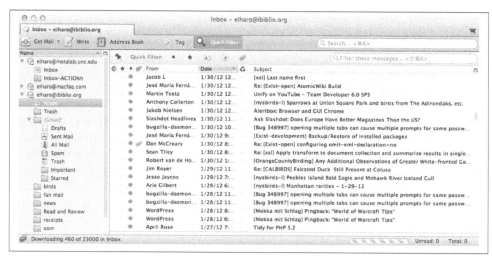

Figure 3-1. A GUI for selecting mail messages

Each of these steps is individually quite simple. The first is to set up the properties for the mail session. Properties you might want to set include `mail.store.protocol`, `mail.pop3.user`, and `mail.pop3.host`:

```
Properties props = new Properties();
props.put("mail.pop3.host", "pop.gmail.com");
props.put("mail.store.protocol", "pop3");
props.put("mail.pop3.user", "erharold");
```

Alternatively you can provide this information in method calls, in which case an empty `Properties` object is enough. Personally I prefer using method arguments instead of system properties when possible since it avoids unexpected, hard-to-debug global configuration problems.

Next, you'll want to create an instance of the `javax.mail.Authenticator` class (more properly, an instance of a concrete subclass of the abstract `Authenticator` class) that can ask the user for a password. For now, we'll simply hardcode those values and pass `null` instead of an actual `Authenticator`:

```
Authenticator a = null;
```

We'll fill this piece in later when we discuss authentication.

Next, use these `Properties` and `Authenticator` objects to get a `Session` instance, like this:

```
Session session = Session.getInstance(props, a);
```

Ask the session for a store for the provider. Here, we want a provider for POP3:

```
Store store = session.getStore("pop3");
```

Finally, you're ready to connect to the store using the `connect()` method. You'll need to provide the host to connect to and the username and password to use:

```
store.connect("mail.cloud9.net", "elharo", "my_password");
```

You can pass `null` for the password to indicate that the previously specified `Authenticator` should be queried for the password.

Now that the store is connected, you're ready to open a folder in the store. This step is really more oriented to IMAP than POP, since POP servers don't keep track of different folders. They simply provide all of a user's incoming mail as one undifferentiated amalgam. For purposes of the JavaMail API, POP3 providers use the folder name INBOX:

```
Folder inbox = store.getFolder("INBOX");
```

The folder is closed when you get it. You can perform some operations on a closed folder including deleting or renaming it, but you can't get the messages out of a closed folder. First you have to open it. You can open a folder for read access by passing the mnemonic constant `Folder.READ_WRITE` to the `open()` method for read access, or `Folder.READ_ONLY` for read/write access:

```
inbox.open(Folder.READ_ONLY);
```

Now you're ready to retrieve the messages with the `getMessages()` method, which returns an array containing pointers to all the messages in the folder:

```
Message[] messages = inbox.getMessages();
```

This call is lazy. That is, it does not actually download the message headers and content. That will be retrieved later when you ask each message for its data.

The `Message` class provides many methods for working with individual messages. It has methods to get the various header fields of the message, get the content of the message, reply to the message, and more. We'll discuss these soon, when we talk about the `Message` and `MimeMessage` classes. For now, we'll do just about the simplest thing imaginable: print each message on `System.out` using the message's `writeTo()` method:

```
for (int i = 0; i < messages.length; i++) {
    System.out.println("------------ Message " + (i+1)
        + " ------------");
    messages[i].writeTo(System.out);
}
```

Once you're done with the messages, close the folder and then close the message store with the aptly named `close()` methods:

```
inbox.close(false);
store.close();
```

The `false` argument to the folder's `close()` method indicates that we do not want the server to actually expunge any deleted messages in the folder. We simply want to break our connection to this folder.

Example 3-1 puts this all together with a basic program that downloads and prints out the contents of a specified POP mailbox. Messages are simply dumped on `System.out` in the default encoding. The servers, usernames, and so forth are all hardcoded. This quickly demonstrates most of the key points of receiving mail with the JavaMail API. A more advanced program would include an appropriate GUI.

Example 3-1. POP3Client

```
import javax.mail.*;
import java.util.*;
import java.io.*;

public class POP3Client {

  public static void main(String[] args) {

    Properties props = new Properties();

    String host = "utopia.poly.edu";
    String username = "eharold";
    String password = "mypassword";
    String provider = "pop3";

    try {
      // Connect to the POP3 server
      Session session = Session.getInstance(props);
      Store store = session.getStore(provider);
      store.connect(host, username, password);
```

```
    // Open the folder
    Folder inbox = store.getFolder("INBOX");
    if (inbox == null) {
      System.out.println("No INBOX");
      System.exit(1);
    }
    inbox.open(Folder.READ_ONLY);

    // Get the messages from the server
    Message[] messages = inbox.getMessages();
    for (int i = 0; i < messages.length; i++) {
      System.out.println("------------ Message " + (i+1)
          + " ------------");
      messages[i].writeTo(System.out);
    }

    // Close the connection
    // but don't remove the messages from the server
    inbox.close(false);
    store.close();
  } catch (MessagingException | IOException ex) {
    ex.printStackTrace();
  }
 }
}
```

Here's some sample output I got when I pointed it at an account I don't use much:

```
$ java POP3Client
------------ Message 1 ------------
Received: (from eharold@localhost)
        by utopia.poly.edu (8.8.8/8.8.8) id QAA05728
        for eharold; Mon, 30 Nov 2009 16:14:29 -0500 (EST)
Date: Mon, 30 Nov 2009 16:14:29 -0500 (EST)
From: Elliotte Harold <eharold@utopia.poly.edu>
Message-Id: <200911302114.QAA05728@utopia.poly.edu>
To: eharold@utopia.poly.edu
Subject: test
Content-Type: text
X-UIDL: 87e3f1ba71738c8f772b15e3933241f0
Status: RO

hello you

------------ Message 2 ------------
Received: from russian.cloud9.net (russian.cloud9.net [
.4])
        by utopia.poly.edu (8.8.8/8.8.8) with ESMTP id OAA28428
        for <eharold@utopia.poly.edu>; Tue, 1 Dec 2009 14:05:06 -0500 (
Received: from [168.100.203.234] (macfaq.dialup.cloud9.net [168.100.203
        by russian.cloud9.net (Postfix) with ESMTP id 24B93764F
        for <eharold@utopia.poly.edu>; Tue, 1 Dec 2009 14:02:50 -0500
Mime-Version: 1.0
```

```
X-Sender: macfaq@mail.cloud9.net
Message-Id: <v04210100b46b1f97969d@[168.100.203.234]>
Date: Tue, 1 Dec 2009 13:55:40 -0500
To: eharold@utopia.poly.edu
From: Elliotte Rusty Harold <elharo@macfaq.com>
Subject: New system
Content-Type: text/plain; charset="us-ascii" ; format="flowed"
X-UIDL: 01fd5cbcf1768fc6c28f9c8f934534b5

Just thought you'd be happy to know that now that I've got my desk
moved over from my old apartment, I've finally ordered the Windows NT
system I've been promising for months.
```

About the only change you'd need to make to port this program to IMAP would be setting the `provider` variable to `imap` instead of `pop3`.

CHAPTER 4

Password Authentication

Hardcoding passwords in source code, as Examples 2-1 and 3-1 do, is a very bad idea to say the least. If a password is required, you should ask the user for it at runtime. Furthermore, when the user types the password, it should not be displayed on the screen. Ideally, it should not even be transmitted in clear text across the network, although in fact many current clients and servers do exactly that.

When you start a mail session, the JavaMail API allows you to provide a `javax.mail.Authenticator` object that it can use to get the username and password. `Authenticator` is an abstract class:

```
public abstract class Authenticator extends Object
```

When the provider needs to know a username or password, it calls back to the `getPasswordAuthentication()` method in a user-defined subclass of `Authenticator`. This returns a `PasswordAuthentication` object containing this information:

```
protected PasswordAuthentication getPasswordAuthentication()
```

 These two classes are almost exactly the same as the `java.net.Authenticator` and `java.net.PasswordAuthentication` classes. Everything you know about `java.net.Authenticator` and `java.net.PasswordAuthentication` is true of `javax.mail.Authenticator` and `javax.mail.PasswordAuthentication`. The only thing you have to watch out for is that if you import both `java.net.*` and `javax.mail.*` in a class, your source code will have to use fully qualified names like `java.net.Authenticator` instead of short names like `Authenticator`.

To add runtime password authentication to your programs, subclass `Authenticator` and override `getPasswordAuthentication()` with a method that knows how to securely ask the user for a password. One useful tool for this process is the JPassword Field component from Swing. Example 4-1 demonstrates a Swing-based Authentica tor subclass that brings up a dialog to ask the user for their username and password.

Example 4-1. A GUI authenticator

```java
import javax.mail.*;
import javax.swing.*;
import java.awt.*;
import java.awt.event.*;

public class MailAuthenticator extends Authenticator {

  private JDialog passwordDialog = new JDialog(new JFrame(), true);
  private JTextField usernameField = new JTextField(20);
  private JPasswordField passwordField = new JPasswordField(20);
  private JButton okButton = new JButton("OK");

  public MailAuthenticator() {
    this("");
  }

  public MailAuthenticator(String username) {
    JLabel mainLabel = new JLabel(
        "Please enter your username and password: ");
    JLabel userLabel = new JLabel("Username: ");
    JLabel passwordLabel = new JLabel("Password: ");

    Container pane = passwordDialog.getContentPane();
    pane.setLayout(new GridLayout(4, 1));
    pane.add(mainLabel);
    JPanel p2 = new JPanel();
    p2.add(userLabel);
    p2.add(usernameField);
    usernameField.setText(username);
    pane.add(p2);
    JPanel p3 = new JPanel();
    p3.add(passwordLabel);
    p3.add(passwordField);
    pane.add(p3);
    JPanel p4 = new JPanel();
    p4.add(okButton);
    pane.add(p4);
    passwordDialog.pack();

    ActionListener listener = new HideDialog();
    okButton.addActionListener(listener);
    usernameField.addActionListener(listener);
    passwordField.addActionListener(listener);
  }

  class HideDialog implements ActionListener {
```

```
  @Override
  public void actionPerformed(ActionEvent event) {
    passwordDialog.setVisible(false);
  }
}

public PasswordAuthentication getPasswordAuthentication() {
  passwordDialog.setVisible(true);

  // getPassword() returns an array of chars for security reasons.
  // We need to convert that to a String for
  // the PasswordAuthentication() constructor.
  String password = new String(passwordField.getPassword());
  String username = usernameField.getText();
  // Erase the password in case this is used again.
  // The provider should cache the password if necessary.
  passwordField.setText("");
  return new PasswordAuthentication(username, password);
}
}
```

Most of this code is just for handling the GUI. Figure 4-1 shows the rather simple dialog box this produces.

Figure 4-1. An authentication dialog

Interestingly, JPasswordField takes more pains to be secure than PasswordAuthenti cation does. JPasswordField stores passwords as an array of chars so that when you're done with the password, you can overwrite it with nulls. This means the password exists in memory for less time and the virtual memory system is less likely to swap the program out to disk and leave the password there in clear text. However, PasswordAuthentica tion stores passwords as strings, which are immutable and therefore are more likely to be written to disk in a VM swap.

Modifying the POP client to support this style of authentication is straightforward, as Example 4-2 demonstrates. We replace the hardcoded username and password with nulls and pass an instance of MailAuthenticator as the second argument to con nect(). The only other change is that we call System.exit() at the end of the main() method, since the program will no longer exit when the main() method returns once the event dispatch thread has been started.

Example 4-2. A POP client that asks the user for the password as necessary

```java
import javax.mail.*;
import java.io.IOException;
import java.util.*;

public class SecurePOP3Client {

  public static void main(String[] args) {
    Properties props = new Properties();
    String host = "utopia.poly.edu";
    String provider = "pop3";

    try {
      // Connect to the POP3 server
      Session session = Session.getInstance(props,
          new MailAuthenticator());
      Store store = session.getStore(provider);
      store.connect(host, null, null);

      // Open the folder
      Folder inbox = store.getFolder("INBOX");
      if (inbox == null) {
        System.out.println("No INBOX");
        System.exit(1);
      }
      inbox.open(Folder.READ_ONLY);

      // Get the messages from the server
      Message[] messages = inbox.getMessages();
      for (int i = 0; i < messages.length; i++) {
        System.out.println("----------- Message " + (i+1)
            + " -----------");
        messages[i].writeTo(System.out);
      }

      // Close the connection
      // but don't remove the messages from the server
      inbox.close(false);
      store.close();
    } catch (MessagingException | IOException ex) {
      ex.printStackTrace();
    }

    // since we brought up a GUI returning from main() won't exit
    System.exit(0);
  }
}
```

CHAPTER 5

Addresses

The `javax.mail.Address` class is very simple. It's an abstract class that exists mainly to be subclassed by other, protocol-specific address classes:

```
public abstract class Address extends Object
```

There are two of these subclasses in the standard JavaMail API: `InternetAddress` for SMTP email and `NewsAddress` for Usenet newsgroups:

```
public class InternetAddress extends Address
public class NewsAddress extends Address
```

Providers of other mail protocols also subclass `Address` with classes that represent their style of address.

The Address Class

The `Address` class itself is extremely simple. It has only three methods, all abstract, two of which are simple utility methods that override the corresponding methods in `java.lang.Object`:

```
public abstract String getType()
public abstract String toString()
public abstract boolean equals(Object o)
```

Since all three of these methods are abstract, there aren't any guarantees about the methods' semantics, since all must be overridden in subclasses. However, this does require that subclasses provide their own implementations of `equals()` and `to String()` rather than relying on the rather generic implementations available from `java.lang.Object` (and as always when you override `equals()` you should override `hashCode()` too). In general, the `getType()` method returns a string such as "rfc822" or "news" that indicates the kind of `Address` object this is.

The InternetAddress Class

An `InternetAddress` object represents an RFC 822-style email address. This is the standard Internet-style email address that is rapidly supplanting all other proprietary formats. It looks like *elharo@ibiblio.org* or *nuts@oreilly.com*. However, it can contain a name as well—for instance, *elharo@ibiblio.org (Elliotte Harold)*.

The state of an `InternetAddress` object is defined by three protected fields:

```
protected String address
protected String personal
protected String encodedPersonal
```

The `address` field is the actual email address—for example, *elharo@ibiblio.org*. The `personal` field is the name—for example, *Elliotte Harold*. Although Java strings are pure Unicode that can express names like Erwin Schrödinger or 孔夫子, the strings used in mail headers must be pure ASCII in order to pass through most existing mail software. Consequently, Java's Unicode strings need to be converted to pure ASCII using a sort of hexadecimal escape. The details of this conversion are described in RFC 2047, *MIME (Multipurpose Internet Mail Extensions) Part Three: Message Header Extensions for Non-ASCII Text*. The encoded string is placed in the `encodedPersonal` field. All of these fields will be initially set in the constructor. There are five overloaded constructors for `InternetAddress` objects:

```
public InternetAddress()
public InternetAddress(String address) throws AddressException
public InternetAddress(String address, boolean strict)
    throws AddressException
public InternetAddress(String address, String personal)
    throws UnsupportedEncodingException
public InternetAddress(String address, String personal, String charset)
    throws UnsupportedEncodingException
```

They are used exactly as you'd expect. For example:

```
Address president = new InternetAddress("president@whitehouse.gov",
    "Barack Obama");
```

Although two of these methods are declared to throw `UnsupportedEncodingExcep tion`, this should happen only in the last method and then only if the name of the character set is not recognized by the VM.

The two constructors declared to throw `AddressException` make basic checks that the string passed is a syntactically correct email address. For instance, they check that the address does not contain white space. However they don't check absolutely everything. If you turn on strict checking, then a couple of other checks are made, primarily that the address contains a domain name as well as a username. Otherwise raw names such as "elharo" are allowed.

There are also three static factory methods that convert a comma-separated string such as `"foo@example.com, bar@example.com"` into an array of addresses:

```
public static InternetAddress[] parse(String addresses)
    throws AddressException
public static InternetAddress[] parse(String address, boolean strict)
    throws AddressException
public static InternetAddress[] parseHeader(String addresses, boolean strict)
    throws AddressException
```

Again all three methods make basic checks that the string passed is a syntactically correct email address. Setting the `strict` argument to `true` makes a couple of extra checks that the regular `parse()` method doesn't. `InternetAddress.parseHeader()` is similar, except in this case setting `strict` argument to `false` makes even fewer checks than the regular `parse()` method.

The `validate()` instance method strictly checks an address that already exists:

```
public void validate() throws AddressException
```

`InternetAddress` objects are mutable. You can change the value of their properties after they are constructed. There are several getter and setter methods:

```
public String getAddress()
public void setAddress(String address)
public String getPersonal()
public void setPersonal(String name) throws UnsupportedEncodingException
public void setPersonal(String name, String charset)
    throws UnsupportedEncodingException
public String getType()
```

The `setAddress()` method sets the `address` field of the object to the specified value. The `setPersonal()` method sets the `personal` and `encodedPersonal` fields to the specified value (after encoding it, as necessary). The `getAddress()` returns the value of the `address` field. The `getPersonal()` method returns the value of the decoded `encodedPersonal` field if it's available, or the `personal` field if it's not. Finally, the `getType()` method returns the string "rfc822".

The `toString()` method returns an email address suitable for use in a To: or From: field of an RFC 822 email message. It encodes non-ASCII characters as specified in RFC 822. The `toUnicodeString()` method does the same except that it leaves non-ASCII characters unencoded:

```
public String toString()
public String toUnicodeString()
```

There are also two unusual static `toString()` methods that convert arrays of addresses to strings:

```
public static String toString(Address[] addresses)
    throws ClassCastException
```

```
public static String toString(Address[] addresses, int used)
    throws ClassCastException
```

The `InternetAddress.toString()` methods convert an array of `Address` objects into a comma-separated list of addresses encoded in pure ASCII, possibly folded onto multiple lines. The optional `used` argument gives the number of characters that will precede this string in the header field, such as To: or Cc:, into which this string will be inserted. This information lets `toString()` decide where it needs to break the lines. A `ClassCastException` is thrown if any of the `Address` objects in the array are not more specifically `InternetAddress` objects.

Finally, the `getLocalAddress()` method checks several system properties (`mail.from`, `mail.user`, `mail.host`, and `user.name`) as well as `InetAddress.getLocalName()` to determine the email address of the current user:

```
public static InternetAddress getLocalAddress(Session session)
```

For example, this code fragment tries to use the user's own email address rather than one hardcoded into the program as a string:

```
msg.setFrom(InternetAddress.getLocalAddress());
```

However, there's no guarantee that any of these properties will necessarily give the user's true address.

The NewsAddress Class

Perhaps a little surprisingly, with an appropriate service provider, the JavaMail API can also access Usenet news. The API is mostly the same as for reading a POP or IMAP mailbox. However, instead of using an `InternetAddress`, you use a `NewsAddress`:

```
public class NewsAddress extends Address
```

A `NewsAddress` object represents a Usenet newsgroup name, such as *comp.lang.java.machine*. It may include the hostname for the news server as well. The state of a `NewsAddress` object is maintained by two protected fields:

```
protected String newsgroup
protected String host
```

The `newsgroup` field contains the name of the newsgroup—for example, *netscape.devs-java*. The `host` field is either null or contains the hostname of the news server—for example, *secnews.netscape.com*. Both of these fields are set in the constructor. There are three overloaded constructors for `NewsAddress` objects:

```
public NewsAddress()
public NewsAddress(String newsgroup)
public NewsAddress(String newsgroup, String host)
```

They are used exactly as you'd expect. For example:

```
Address recHumorFunny = new NewsAddress("rec.humor.funny",
    "nntp.aioe.org");
```

There are eight instance methods in this class—three getter methods, two setter methods, and three utility methods:

```
public String  getType()
public String  getHost()
public String  getNewsgroup()
public void    setNewsgroup(String newsgroup)
public void    setHost(String host)
public String  toString()
public boolean equals(Object o)
public int     hashCode()
```

The setNewsgroup() and setHost() methods set the newsgroup and host fields of the object to the specified values. The getNewsgroup() and getHost() methods return the values of the newsgroup and host fields. Finally, the getType() method returns the string "news".

The toString() method returns the newsgroup name in a form suitable for the Newsgroups: header field of a Usenet posting. The equals() and hashCode() methods have their usual semantics.

There are also two static utility methods for converting addresses to and from strings:

```
public static String toString(Address[] addresses)
    throws ClassCastException
public static NewsAddress[] parse(String newsgroups)
    throws AddressException
```

The toString() method converts an array of Address objects into a comma-separated list of newsgroup names. A ClassCastException is thrown if any of the Address objects in the array are not more specifically NewsAddress objects. The parse() method reverses this operation, converting a comma-separated String of newsgroup names, such as "comp.lang.java.programmer,comp.lang.java.gui,comp.lang.java.help", into an array of NewsAddress objects. It throws an AddressException if the newsgroups argument is not a comma-separated list of newsgroup names.

The reference implementation of the JavaMail API does not include a service provider for news, however; although you can create news addresses, before you can actually read and post news you'll need to install a service provider that supports it. Table 1-1 lists some possible sources of news providers. Once you've got one, reading news is as straightforward as talking to an IMAP server.

CHAPTER 6

The URLName Class

`javax.mail.URLName` treats a URL as a string, but does not attempt to connect to or resolve any of the parts of the string. It's conceptually similar to `java.net.URI` but predates it by several years.

URL names are mainly used as convenient ways to identify folders and stores with nonstandard URLs (such as *pop3://elharo:mypassword@mail.ibiblio.org:110/INBOX*) that don't have a matching protocol handler:

```
public class URLName Object
```

The methods of `URLName` are very similar to those of `java.net.URL`, except that all those involving actual connections have been deleted. What's left is a bunch of methods for breaking a URL string into its component parts or building a URL from pieces.

The Constructors

There are three overloaded `URLName` constructors. One takes the individual pieces of a URL as arguments, another takes a `java.net.URL` object, and a third takes a `String` containing a URL:

```
public URLName(String protocol, String host, int port, String file,
    String userName, String password)
public URLName(URL url)
public URLName(String url)
```

All the operations on the `URLName` take place with simple substring manipulation, allowing the `URLName` class to support nonstandard URLs such as pop3://eharold:password@utopia.poly.edu/INBOX or imap://elharo@ibiblio.org/Speaking/SD2008West. These `URLName` objects can be used to refer to particular folders on the server.

Parsing Methods

These seven getter methods are the main purpose for this class. They return individual pieces of the URL:

```
public int    getPort()
public String getProtocol()
public String getFile()
public String getRef()
public String getHost()
public String getUsername()
public String getPassword()
```

These methods can all be easily understood by analogy with the similarly named methods in `java.net.URL`. Except for `getPort()`, these methods all return `null` if the piece is missing. `getPort()` returns -1 if the port is not explicitly included in the URL.

There's also a `getURL()` method that converts a `URLName` to a `java.net.URL`. Since doing so requires that Java have a protocol handler for the URL's scheme, this method can throw a `MalformedURLException`:

```
public URL getURL() throws MalformedURLException
```

Finally, there are the usual three utility methods with the usual semantics:

```
public boolean equals(Object o)
public int     hashCode()
public String  toString()
```

The `toString()` method simply returns the string form of the URL. The `equals()` method is underspecified but in practice any two `URLName` objects that are character-by-character identical will compare equal. However, JavaMail does not consider case to be significant in domain names. `http://www.example.com` and `http://WWW.EXAM PLE.COM` are equal. Surprisingly, it does consider case to be significant in URL schemes. That is, `http://www.example.com` is not equal to `HTTP://www.example.com`. Finally, JavaMail recognizes / as the default path; for example, `http://www.example.com` is equal to `http://www.example.com/`. The `hashCode()` method is implemented accordingly.

We can use the `URLName` class to provide an interface for an email client that is completely protocol-independent. All information about protocol, host, and other details is provided by a URL read from the command line. Example 6-1 demonstrates.

Example 6-1. A protocol-independent mail client

```
import javax.mail.*;
import java.io.IOException;
import java.util.*;

public class MailClient {
```

```
  public static void main(String[] args) {
    if (args.length == 0) {
      System.err.println(
          "Usage: java MailClient protocol://username:password@host/foldername");
      return;
    }

    URLName server = new URLName(args[0]);

    try {
      Session session = Session.getInstance(new Properties());

      // Connect to the server and open the folder
      Folder folder = session.getFolder(server);
      if (folder == null) {
        System.out.println("Folder " + server.getFile() + " not found.");
        System.exit(1);
      }
      folder.open(Folder.READ_ONLY);

      // Get the messages from the server
      Message[] messages = folder.getMessages();
      for (int i = 0; i < messages.length; i++) {
        System.out.println("------------ Message " + (i+1)
            + " ------------");
        messages[i].writeTo(System.out);
      }

      // Close the connection
      // but don't remove the messages from the server
      folder.close(false);
    } catch (IOException | MessagingException ex) {
      ex.printStackTrace();
    }
  }
}
```

URLName does make the code a little more compact since it moves some information
from the source code to the command line. Besides eliminating the obvious variables
and string literals for username, host, and so forth, we've managed to eliminate any
direct reference to the Store class. A typical run starts like this:

```
% java MailClient pop3://eharold:mypassword@utopia.poly.edu/INBOX
------------ Message 1 ------------
Received: (from eharold@localhost)
        by utopia.poly.edu (8.8.8/8.8.8) id QAA05728
        for eharold; Mon, 30 Nov 2009 16:14:29 -0500 (EST)
Date: Mon, 30 Nov 2009 16:14:29 -0500 (EST)
From: Elliotte Harold <eharold@utopia.poly.edu>
Message-Id: <200911302114.QAA05728@utopia.poly.edu>
To: eharold@utopia.poly.edu
```

```
Subject: test
Content-Type: text
X-UIDL: 87e3f1ba71738c8f772b15e3933241f0
Status: RO

hello you
```

For demonstration purposes, this program includes the password in the URL. In general, however, that's a huge security risk. It would be much better to use a runtime Authenticator.

CHAPTER 7

Messages and Parts

The `javax.mail.Message` class is the abstract superclass for all individual emails, news postings, and similar messages:

```
public abstract class Message extends Object implements Part
```

There's one concrete `Message` subclass in the standard JavaMail API, `javax.mail.internet.MimeMessage`. This is used for both email and Usenet news messages. Service providers are free to add classes for their own message formats. For instance, IBM might provide a `NotesMessage` class for IBM Notes.

The `Message` class mainly declares abstract getter and setter methods that define the common properties of most messages. These properties include the addressees of the message, the recipients of the message, the subject and content of the message, and various other attributes. You can think of these as properties of the envelope that contains the message.

Furthermore, the `Message` class implements the `Part` interface. The `Part` interface mostly handles the body of an email message. It declares methods for getting and setting the content type of the message body, getting and setting the actual message body content, getting and setting arbitrary headers from the message, and getting input streams that are fed by the message body. The main body part of a message can contain other parts. This is used to handle attachments, message bodies that are available in multiple formats, and other multipart emails. Since the `Message` class is abstract and needs to be subclassed by concrete classes such as `MimeMessage`, most of these methods are not actually redeclared in `Message` but can be invoked by any actual instance of `Message`. We'll begin by discussing the methods actually declared in `Message`, then move on to those declared in `Part`.

Creating Messages

The `Message` class has three constructors:

```
protected Message()
protected Message(Folder folder, int messageNumber)
protected Message(Session session)
```

Since all the constructors are protected, they are primarily for the use of subclasses such as `MimeMessage`. If you're sending a message, you'll use one of the constructors in the subclass instead. If you're reading messages, the `Folder` or `Session` you're reading from will create the `Message` objects and pass them to you.

Replying to Messages

If you already have a `Message` object, one way to create a new `Message` object is to reply to the existing one using the `reply()` method:

```
public abstract Message reply(boolean replyToAll)
    throws MessagingException
```

This method creates a new `Message` object with the same subject prefixed with "Re:", and addressed to the sender of the original message. If `replyToAll` is `true`, the message is addressed to all known recipients of the original message. The content of the message is empty. If you want to quote the original message, you'll have to do that yourself.

Getting Messages from Folders

You've already seen that when you're reading email, the JavaMail API creates `Message` objects to represent the messages it finds on the server. The primary means of doing this are the `getMessage()` and `getMessages()` methods in the `Folder` class:

```
public abstract Message getMessage(int messageNumber)
    throws MessagingException
public Message[] getMessages(int start, int end)
    throws MessagingException
public Message[] getMessages(int[] messageNumbers)
    throws MessagingException
public Message[] getMessages() throws MessagingException
```

The first three methods require the caller to specify which messages it wants. The last simply returns all messages in the folder. What's actually returned are stubs holding the places of the actual messages. The text and headers of the message won't necessarily be retrieved until some method of the `Message` class is invoked that requires this information.

Basic Header Info

A typical RFC 822 message contains a header that looks something like this:

```
From levi@blazing.sunspot.noao.edu Tue Aug 5 10:57:08 2014
Date: Tue, 27 Aug 2014 10:57:04 +0700
From: levi@blazing.sunspot.noao.edu (Denise Levi)
To: volleyball@sunspot.noao.edu
Subject: Apologies
Content-Length: 517
Status: RO
X-Lines: 13
```

The exact fields in the header can vary, but most messages contain at least a From: field, a To: field, a Date: field, and a Subject: field. Other common fields include Cc: (carbon copies) and Bcc: (blind carbon copies). In general, these will be accessible through getter and setter methods.

The From Address

These four methods get and set the From: field of a message:

```
public abstract Address[] getFrom() throws MessagingException
public abstract void setFrom() throws MessagingException,
    IllegalWriteException, IllegalStateException
public abstract void setFrom(Address address)
    throws MessagingException, IllegalWriteException, IllegalStateException
public abstract void addFrom(Address[] addresses)
    throws MessagingException, IllegalWriteException, IllegalStateException
```

The getFrom() method returns an array of Address objects, one for each address listed in the From: header. (In practice, it's rare for a message to be *from* more than one address. It's quite common for a message to be addressed *to* more than one address.) It returns null if the From: header isn't present in the message. It throws a MessagingException if the From: header is malformed in some way.

The noargs setFrom() and addFrom() methods set and modify the From: headers of outgoing email messages. The noargs setFrom() method sets the header to the current value of the mail.user property or, as a fallback, the user.name property. The set From() method with arguments sets the value of the From: header to the listed addresses. The addFrom() method adds the listed addresses to any addresses that already exist in the header. All three of these methods can throw a MessagingException if one of the addresses they use isn't in the right format. They can also throw an Illegal WriteException if the From: field of the given Message object cannot be changed or an IllegalStateException if the entire Message object is read-only.

If the message object is more specifically a `MimeMessage` object, there is also a set From() method that takes a `String` as an argument, so you don't have to first construct an `Address` object:

```
public void setFrom(String address)
    throws MessagingException, IllegalWriteException, IllegalStateException
```

The Reply-to Address

Some messages contain a Reply-to: header indicating that any replies should be sent to a different address than the one that sent the message. There are two methods to set and get these addresses:

```
public Address[] getReplyTo() throws MessagingException
public void setReplyTo(Address[] addresses) throws MessagingException,
    MethodNotSupportedException, IllegalWriteException,
    IllegalStateException
```

The semantics of these methods are the same as for the equivalent getFrom() and setFrom() methods—in fact, the default implementation of getReplyTo() simply returns getFrom()—with the single caveat that an implementation that doesn't support separate Reply-to: addresses may throw a `MethodNotSupportedException` when setReplyTo() is invoked.

The Recipient Addresses

Whereas the sender of the message is generally found only in the From: header, the recipients of the message are often split across the To:, Cc:, and Bcc: fields. Rather than providing separate methods for each of these fields, the various getRecipients() and setRecipients() methods rely on a `Message.RecipientType` argument to determine which field's value is desired. `RecipientType` is a public inner class in `jav ax.mail.Message` whose private constructor limits it to exactly these three static objects:

```
Message.RecipientType.TO
Message.RecipientType.CC
Message.RecipientType.BCC
```

There are two methods to find the addressees of the `Message`:

```
public abstract Address[] getRecipients(Message.RecipientType type)
  throws MessagingException
public Address[] getAllRecipients() throws MessagingException
```

The getRecipients() method returns an array of Address objects, one for each address listed in the specified header. It returns null if the specified header isn't present in the message. It throws a `MessagingException` if the specified header is malformed in some way. The getAllRecipients() method does the same thing, except that it combines the contents of the To:, Cc:, and Bcc: headers.

There are two methods to set the recipients of the message while replacing any previous recipients and two methods to add recipients to the message:

```
public abstract void setRecipients(Message.RecipientType type,
    Address[] addresses) throws MessagingException, IllegalWriteException,
    IllegalStateException
public void setRecipient(Message.RecipientType type, Address address)
    throws MessagingException, IllegalWriteException
public abstract void addRecipients(Message.RecipientType type,
    Address[] addresses) throws MessagingException,
    IllegalWriteException, IllegalStateException
public void addRecipient(Message.RecipientType type, Address address)
    throws MessagingException, IllegalWriteException
```

All four of these methods can throw a `MessagingException`, typically because one of the addresses isn't in the right format. They can also throw an `IllegalWriteException` if the specified field of the given `Message` object cannot be changed or an `IllegalStateException` if the entire `Message` object is read-only.

The Subject of the Message

Since the subject is simply a single string of text, it's easy to get and set with these two methods:

```
public abstract String getSubject() throws MessagingException
public abstract void    setSubject(String subject) throws
    MessagingException, IllegalWriteException, IllegalStateException
```

As with earlier setter methods, the getter returns `null` if the subject field isn't present in the message. The setter throws an `IllegalWriteException` if the program isn't allowed to set the value of the Subject: field and an `IllegalStateException` if the program isn't allowed to change the message at all.

The Date of the Message

Messages also have sent and received dates. Three methods allow programs to access these fields:

```
public abstract Date getSentDate() throws MessagingException
public abstract void setSentDate(Date date) throws MessagingException,
    IllegalWriteException, IllegalStateException
public abstract Date getReceivedDate() throws MessagingException
```

The underlying implementation is responsible for converting the textual date format found in a message header like "Wed, 20 Aug 2014 10:57:04 0700" to a `java.util.Date` object. As usual, a `MessagingException` indicates some problem with the format of the underlying message, an `IllegalWriteException` indicates that the field cannot be changed, and an `IllegalStateException` indicates that the entire message cannot be changed.

Example 7-1 is a simple example program that follows the basic pattern of the last several mail-reading programs. However, this one no longer uses writeTo(). Instead, it uses the methods in this section to print just the headers. Furthermore, it prints them in a particular order regardless of their order in the actual message on the server. Finally, it ignores the less important headers such as X-UIDL: and Status:. The static InternetAddress.toString() method converts the arrays that most of these methods return into simple, comma-separated strings.

Example 7-1. A program to read mail headers

```java
import javax.mail.*;
import javax.mail.internet.*;
import java.util.*;

public class HeaderClient {

  public static void main(String[] args) {
    if (args.length == 0) {
      System.err.println(
          "Usage: java HeaderClient protocol://username@host/foldername");
      return;
    }

    URLName server = new URLName(args[0]);

    try {
      Session session = Session.getInstance(new Properties(),
          new MailAuthenticator(server.getUsername()));

      // Connect to the server and open the folder
      Folder folder = session.getFolder(server);
      if (folder == null) {
        System.out.println("Folder " + server.getFile() + " not found.");
        System.exit(1);
      }
      folder.open(Folder.READ_ONLY);

      // Get the messages from the server
      Message[] messages = folder.getMessages();
      for (int i = 0; i < messages.length; i++) {
        System.out.println("------------ Message " + (i+1)
            + " ------------");
        // Here's the big change...
        String from = InternetAddress.toString(messages[i].getFrom());
        if (from != null) System.out.println("From: " + from);
        String replyTo = InternetAddress.toString(
            messages[i].getReplyTo());
        if (replyTo != null) System.out.println("Reply-to: "
            + replyTo);
        String to = InternetAddress.toString(
            messages[i].getRecipients(Message.RecipientType.TO));
```

```
        if (to != null) System.out.println("To: " + to);
        String cc = InternetAddress.toString(
            messages[i].getRecipients(Message.RecipientType.CC));
        if (cc != null) System.out.println("Cc: " + cc);
        String bcc = InternetAddress.toString(
            messages[i].getRecipients(Message.RecipientType.BCC));
        if (bcc != null) System.out.println("Bcc: " + bcc);
        String subject = messages[i].getSubject();
        if (subject != null) System.out.println("Subject: " + subject);
            Date sent = messages[i].getSentDate();
        if (sent != null) System.out.println("Sent: " + sent);
        Date received = messages[i].getReceivedDate();
        if (received != null) System.out.println("Received: " + received);

        System.out.println();
      }

      // Close the connection
      // but don't remove the messages from the server
      folder.close(false);
    } catch (MessagingException ex) {
      ex.printStackTrace();
    }

    // Since we may have brought up a GUI to authenticate,
    // we can't rely on returning from main() to exit
    System.exit(0);
  }
}
```

Here's some typical output. Several of the requested strings were null because the fields simply weren't present in the messages in the INBOX; for instance, Cc: and Bcc:. Head erClient checks for the fields and simply omits them if they're not present.

```
% java HeaderClient pop3://eharold@utopia.poly.edu/INBOX
------------ Message 1 ------------
From: Elliotte Harold <eharold@utopia.poly.edu>
Reply-to: Elliotte Harold <eharold@utopia.poly.edu>
To: eharold@utopia.poly.edu
Subject: test
Sent: Mon Nov 30 13:14:29 PST 2009

------------ Message 2 ------------
From: Elliotte Rusty Harold <elharo@macfaq.com>
Reply-to: Elliotte Rusty Harold <elharo@macfaq.com>
To: eharold@utopia.poly.edu
Subject: New system
Sent: Tue Dec 01 10:55:40 PST 2009

------------ Message 3 ------------
From: Dr. Mickel <Greatsmiles@mail.com>
Reply-to: Dr. Mickel <Greatsmiles@mail.com>
```

```
To: eharold@utopia.poly.edu
Subject: Breath RX Products now available Online!
Sent: Wed Dec 02 03:45:52 PST 2009
```

Notice that none of these messages have received dates. That's because the receive time is not part of the message envelope itself. It has to be provided by the server, and POP servers don't provide it. An IMAP server would be much more likely to include a received date, as will be shown in Example 7-2.

Flags

Mail programs can save extra information about the messages that are not part of the messages themselves. For instance, Pine lets me know whether I've replied to or read a message, and so on. As Figure 7-1 shows, this information is indicated by symbols and letters in the lefthand column. D means a message has been deleted; A means it's been answered; N is a new message that hasn't been read yet; and so forth. In the JavaMail API, these are all represented as *flags*. A flag is an instance of the `javax.mail.Flags` class:

```
public class Flags extends Object implements Cloneable
```

Seven flags are predefined as instances of the public static inner class `Flags.Flag`. These are:

```
Flags.Flag.ANSWERED
Flags.Flag.DELETED
Flags.Flag.DRAFT
Flags.Flag.FLAGGED
Flags.Flag.RECENT
Flags.Flag.SEEN
Flags.Flag.USER
```

In addition, some implementations may allow arbitrary user-defined flags. If so, the USER flag is set.

Figure 7-1. Pine shows flags as letters in the lefthand column

The `getFlags()` method returns the flags of a particular message:

```
public abstract Flags getFlags() throws MessagingException
```

The `isSet()` method tests whether a specified flag is set for the given message:

```
public boolean isSet(Flags.Flag flag) throws MessagingException
```

Finally, the `setFlags()` and `setFlag()` methods set or unset (depending on the second argument) the flag indicated by the first argument:

```
public abstract void setFlags(Flags flag, boolean set)
    throws MessagingException, IllegalWriteException,
    IllegalStateException
public void setFlag(Flags.Flag flag, boolean set) throws
    MessagingException, IllegalWriteException, IllegalStateException
```

You delete messages by setting their `Flags.Flag.DELETED` flag to `true`. For example, to delete `message`:

```
message.setFlag(Flags.Flag.DELETED, true);
```

This only marks the message as deleted. It does not actually expunge it from the file on the server. Until the message is expunged, it can still be undeleted by setting `Flags.Flag.DELETED` back to `false`.

Example 7-2 is a slight modification of Example 7-1, `HeaderClient`, which prints the flags as well. As a general rule, POP servers won't report flags. Only a protocol that stores messages and forwards them, such as IMAP or mbox, will report flags.

Example 7-2. A program to read mailbox flags

```
import javax.mail.*;
import javax.mail.internet.*;
import java.util.*;

public class FlagsClient {

  public static void main(String[] args) {
    if (args.length == 0) {
      System.err.println(
          "Usage: java FlagsClient protocol://username@host/foldername");
      return;
    }

    URLName server = new URLName(args[0]);

    try {
      Session session = Session.getInstance(new Properties(),
          new MailAuthenticator(server.getUsername()));

      // Connect to the server and open the folder
      Folder folder = session.getFolder(server);
```

```
if (folder == null) {
  System.out.println("Folder " + server.getFile() + " not found.");
  System.exit(1);
}
folder.open(Folder.READ_ONLY);

// Get the messages from the server
Message[] messages = folder.getMessages();
for (int i = 0; i < messages.length; i++) {
  System.out.println("----------- Message " + (i+1)
      + " -----------");
  // Get the headers
  String from = InternetAddress.toString(messages[i].getFrom());
  if (from != null) System.out.println("From: " + from);
  String replyTo = InternetAddress.toString(
      messages[i].getReplyTo());
  if (replyTo != null) System.out.println("Reply-to: " + replyTo);
  String to = InternetAddress.toString(
      messages[i].getRecipients(Message.RecipientType.TO));
  if (to != null) System.out.println("To: " + to);
  String cc = InternetAddress.toString(
      messages[i].getRecipients(Message.RecipientType.CC));
  if (cc != null) System.out.println("Cc: " + cc);
  String bcc = InternetAddress.toString(
      messages[i].getRecipients(Message.RecipientType.BCC));
  if (bcc != null) System.out.println("Bcc: " + bcc);
  String subject = messages[i].getSubject();
  if (subject != null) System.out.println("Subject: " + subject);
  Date sent = messages[i].getSentDate();
  if (sent != null) System.out.println("Sent: " + sent);
  Date received = messages[i].getReceivedDate();
  if (received != null) System.out.println("Received: " + received);

  // Now test the flags:
  if (messages[i].isSet(Flags.Flag.DELETED)) {
    System.out.println("Deleted");
  }
  if (messages[i].isSet(Flags.Flag.ANSWERED)) {
    System.out.println("Answered");
  }
  if (messages[i].isSet(Flags.Flag.DRAFT)) {
    System.out.println("Draft");
  }
  if (messages[i].isSet(Flags.Flag.FLAGGED)) {
    System.out.println("Marked");
  }
  if (messages[i].isSet(Flags.Flag.RECENT)) {
    System.out.println("Recent");
  }
  if (messages[i].isSet(Flags.Flag.SEEN)) {
    System.out.println("Read");
  }
```

```
      if (messages[i].isSet(Flags.Flag.USER)) {
        // We don't know what the user flags might be in advance
        // so they're returned as an array of strings
        String[] userFlags = messages[i].getFlags().getUserFlags();
        for (String flag : userFlags) {
          System.out.println("User flag: " +  flag);
        }
      }
      System.out.println();
    }

    // Close the connection
    // but don't remove the messages from the server
    folder.close(false);
  } catch (MessagingException ex) {
    ex.printStackTrace();
  }

  // Since we may have brought up a GUI to authenticate,
  // we can't rely on returning from main() to exit
  System.exit(0);
  }
}
```

Here's a sample run. The first message has been read and deleted. The second message has no set flags; it hasn't been read, deleted, or answered. The third message has been read and answered but not deleted. Notice that I'm using an IMAP server instead of a POP server:

```
% java FlagsClient imap://elharo@mail.ibiblio.org/INBOX
------------ Message 1 ------------
From: Mike Hall <mikehall@spacestar.com>
Reply-to: Mike Hall <mikehall@spacestar.com>
To: mrj-dev@public.lists.apple.com
Subject: Re: dialog box, parents & X-platform
Sent: Sun Dec 13 05:24:38 PST 2009
Received: Sun Dec 13 06:33:00 PST 2009
Deleted
Read

------------ Message 2 ------------
From: Kapil Madan <kapil.madan@MIT-MISYS.COM>
Reply-to: XML-INTEREST@JAVA.SUN.COM
To: XML-INTEREST@JAVA.SUN.COM
Subject: Re: first mail to the list!
Sent: Sun Dec 13 06:19:46 PST 2009
Received: Sun Dec 13 06:40:00 PST 2009

------------ Message 3 ------------
From: Jim Jackl-Mochel <jmochel@foliage.com>
Reply-to: Jim Jackl-Mochel <jmochel@foliage.com>
To: elharo@ibiblio.org
```

```
Subject: CPreProcessorStream
Sent: Sun Dec 13 07:14:00 PST 2009
Received: Sun Dec 13 07:08:00 PST 2009
Answered
Read
```

Folders

Messages received from the network (as opposed to sent to the network) generally belong to some Folder. The getFolder() method returns a reference to the Folder object that contains this Message:

```
public Folder getFolder()
```

It returns null if the message isn't contained in a folder.

Within a folder, messages are organized from first (message 1) to last. The getMessage Number() method returns the relative position of this Message in its Folder:

```
public int getMessageNumber()
```

Messages that aren't in any folder have number 0.

One of the things you can do with a folder is expunge messages from it. This physically deletes the message if it's already been marked as deleted. (A merely deleted message can be "undeleted", whereas an expunged message cannot be.) If a message is expunged, there may still be a Message object pointing to the message, but almost all methods on the message will throw a MessagingException. Thus, it may be important to check whether a message has been expunged before working with it. The isExpunged() method does that:

```
public boolean isExpunged()
```

Searching

The final method left in the Message class is match(). The match() method determines whether a Message satisfies particular search criteria. We'll discuss this more in a bit when we talk about searching folders:

```
public boolean match(SearchTerm term) throws MessagingException
```

The Part Interface

Both Message and BodyPart implement the Part interface. Every Message is a Part. However, some parts may contain other parts. The Part interface declares three kinds of methods:

- Methods for getting and setting the attributes of the part

- Methods for getting and setting the headers of the part
- Methods for getting and setting the contents of the part

The attributes of the part are details that aren't explicitly specified in the message's header, such as the size of the message or the date it was received. The headers, by contrast, are name-value pairs included at the front of the part. Finally, the content of the part is the actual data that the message is trying to transmit.

Attributes

The JavaMail API defines five attributes for parts:

Size
> The approximate number of bytes in the part

Line count
> The number of lines in the part

Disposition
> Whether the part is an attachment or should be displayed in-line

Description
> A brief text summary of the part

Filename
> The name of the file that the attachment came from

Not all parts have all attributes. For instance, a part that does not represent an attached file is unlikely to have a filename attribute. Each attribute is mapped to a getter method:

```
public int    getSize() throws MessagingException
public int    getLineCount() throws MessagingException
public String getDisposition() throws MessagingException
public String getDescription() throws MessagingException
public String getFileName() throws MessagingException, ParseException
```

Generally, each getter method returns null or -1 if a part doesn't possess the requested attribute. It throws a MessagingException if there's some problem retrieving the message; for instance, if the connection goes down while the message is being retrieved.

The getSize() method returns the approximate number of bytes in the part. Depending on the server and protocol, this may or may not account for changes in the size caused by operations such as Base64 encoding the data.

The getLineCount() method returns the approximate number of lines in the content of the part or -1 if the number of lines isn't known. Again, the number returned may or may not account for changes in the size of the part caused by the part's encoding.

The `getDisposition()` method returns a string indicating whether the content should be presented in-line or as an attachment. The value returned should either be `null` (the disposition is not known) or one of the two named constants, `Part.INLINE` or `Part.ATTACHMENT`:

```
public static final String ATTACHMENT = "attachment";
public static final String INLINE     = "inline";
```

If the disposition is `Part.ATTACHMENT`, `getFileName()` should return the name of the file to save the attachment in. Otherwise, `getFileName()` probably returns `null`. However, some email clients do not properly set the Content-disposition header for attachments. Consequently, when receiving messages with attachments, you'll often get a `null` disposition but a non-null filename. In practice, it seems more reliable to assume that any body part with a non-null filename is an attachment regardless of the Content-disposition header, and any body part with no filename and no Content-disposition header should be displayed in-line if possible. If it's not possible—for instance, if you can't handle the MIME type—you can either ask the user for a filename or pick some reasonable default, such as *attachment1.tif*.

Normally, the filename includes only the actual name of the file but not any of the directories the file was in. It's up to the application receiving the message to decide where to put the incoming file. For instance, Thunderbird generally stores attachments in the Downloads folder inside the user's home directory or on the desktop. However, the user has an option to pick a different location.

You need to be careful before using a filename that arrives in an email message. In particular make sure you escape or remove any illegal characters or hierarchy delimiters such as /. Different systems have different rules for file names so what's a legal file name on Windows may not be on a Mac, and vice versa.

Furthermore, since it's not uncommon to receive multiple attachments with the same name over time, check to see whether a file with the attached file's name already exists before writing out the attachment. If a similarly named file does exist, you'll have to rename the attachment in some reasonable fashion—for instance, by appending a 1 or a 2 to it: e.g., *vcard1.vcf*, *vcard2.vcf*, and so on.

The description, disposition, and filename attributes also have setter methods. However, the size and line count attributes are determined by the content of the part rather than a setter method:

```
public void setDisposition(String disposition) throws
    MessagingException, IllegalWriteException, IllegalStateException
public void setFileName(String filename) throws MessagingException,
    IllegalWriteException, IllegalStateException
public void setDescription(String description) throws
    MessagingException, IllegalWriteException, IllegalStateException
```

The setter methods all throw a MessagingException if there's some problem while changing the message. They can also throw an IllegalWriteException if the relevant attribute of the part cannot be modified or an IllegalStateException if the part belongs to a read-only folder.

The setDisposition() method determines whether the part is to be viewed in-line or as an attachment. Although it's declared to take a String as an argument, this String should be one of the two named constants, Part.INLINE or Part.ATTACHMENT. Parts that are attachments generally have a filename included in their metainformation. This name can be set with the setFileName() method. Finally, the setDescription() method can take any String at all to add a description to the part.

Example 7-3 is a simple program that connects to a mail server and reads the attributes of the messages in the mailbox. Since each message is itself a part (even if it contains other parts), we can invoke these methods on the entire message.

Example 7-3. A program to read mail attributes

```java
import javax.mail.*;
import javax.mail.internet.*;
import java.util.*;

public class AttributeClient {

  public static void main(String[] args) {
    if (args.length == 0) {
      System.err.println(
          "Usage: java AttributeClient protocol://username@host/foldername");
      return;
    }

    URLName server = new URLName(args[0]);
    try {
      Session session = Session.getInstance(new Properties(),
          new MailAuthenticator(server.getUsername()));

      // Connect to the server and open the folder
      Folder folder = session.getFolder(server);
      if (folder == null) {
        System.out.println("Folder " + server.getFile() + " not found.");
        System.exit(1);
      }
      folder.open(Folder.READ_ONLY);

      // Get the messages from the server
      Message[] messages = folder.getMessages();
      for (int i = 0; i < messages.length; i++) {
        System.out.println("------------ Message " + (i+1)
            + " ------------");
        String from = InternetAddress.toString(messages[i].getFrom());
```

```
        if (from != null) System.out.println("From: " + from);
        String to = InternetAddress.toString(
            messages[i].getRecipients(Message.RecipientType.TO));
        if (to != null) System.out.println("To: " + to);
        String subject = messages[i].getSubject();
        if (subject != null) System.out.println("Subject: " + subject);
        Date sent = messages[i].getSentDate();
        if (sent != null) System.out.println("Sent: " + sent);

        System.out.println();
        // Here's the attributes...
        System.out.println("This message is approximately "
            + messages[i].getSize() + " bytes long.");
        System.out.println("This message has approximately "
            + messages[i].getLineCount() + " lines.");
        String disposition = messages[i].getDisposition();
        if (disposition == null) ; // do nothing
        else if (disposition.equals(Part.INLINE)) {
          System.out.println("This part should be displayed inline");
        } else if (disposition.equals(Part.ATTACHMENT)) {
          System.out.println("This part is an attachment");
          String fileName = messages[i].getFileName();
          if (fileName != null) {
            System.out.println("The file name of this attachment is "
                + fileName);
          }
        }
        String description = messages[i].getDescription();
        if (description != null) {
          System.out.println("The description of this message is "
              + description);
        }
      }

      // Close the connection
      // but don't remove the messages from the server
      folder.close(false);
    } catch (MessagingException ex) {
      ex.printStackTrace();
    }

    // Since we may have brought up a GUI to authenticate,
    // we can't rely on returning from main() to exit
    System.exit(0);
  }
}
```

Here's some typical output. I used an IMAP server because most of these methods don't work nearly as well with POP servers. IMAP servers can give you the attributes of a message without making you download the entire message, but POP servers aren't that sophisticated:

```
% java AttributeClient imap://elharo@mail.ibiblio.org/INBOX
------------ Message 1 ------------
From: "Richman, Jeremy" <jrichman@hq.ileaf.com>
To: 'xsl-list' <XSL-List@mulberrytech.com>
Subject: Re: New twist: eliminating nodes with duplicate content
Sent: Thu Dec 06 08:37:51 PST 2012

This message is approximately 3391 bytes long.
This message has approximately 87 lines.
------------ Message 2 ------------
From: schererm@us.ibm.com
To: Unicode List <unicode@unicode.org>
Subject: Re: Number ordering
Sent: Thu Dec 06 11:00:28 PST 2012

This message is approximately 1554 bytes long.
This message has approximately 18 lines.
------------ Message 3 ------------
From: John Posner <jjp@connix.com>
To: 'Nakita Watson' <nakita@oreilly.com>
Subject: RE: Another conference Call
Sent: Thu Dec 06 11:16:38 PST 2012
This message is approximately 1398 bytes long.
This message has approximately 19 lines.
```

Headers

Classes that implement the Part interface—for example, Message—generally declare methods to return specific headers such as To: or From:. The Part interface, by contrast, declares methods to get and set arbitrary headers regardless of name.

The getHeader() method gets the values of all the headers with a name that matches the name argument. Some headers such as Received: can have multiple values and can be included in a message multiple times, so this method returns those values as an array of strings. It returns null if no header with that name is present in this Part:

```
public String[] getHeader(String name) throws MessagingException
```

The setHeader() method adds a new header to an outgoing message:

```
public void setHeader(String name, String value) throws
    MessagingException, IllegalWriteException, IllegalStateException
```

If there's already a header with this name, that header is deleted and the new one inserted in its place—unless the folder in which the message resides is read-only, in which case an IllegalStateException is thrown.

By contrast, the addHeader() method adds a header with the specified name without replacing any that already exist:

```
public void addHeader(String name, String value) throws
    MessagingException, IllegalWriteException, IllegalStateException
```

The removeHeader() method deletes all instances of the named header from this Part:

```
public void removeHeader(String name) throws MessagingException,
    IllegalWriteException, IllegalStateException
```

The getAllHeaders() method returns a java.util.Enumeration object containing all the headers in this message:

```
public Enumeration getAllHeaders() throws MessagingException
```

This method is annoyingly non-generic, and you'll want to suppress generics warnings.

The Enumeration contains one javax.mail.Header object for each header in the message:

```
public class Header extends Object
```

The Header class is very simple, with just a constructor to set the name and value of the header, and getName() and getValue() methods to return them:

```
public Header(String name, String value)
public String getName()
public String getValue()
```

Finally, the getMatchingHeaders() method returns an Enumeration containing all the headers in this message with names that are one of the strings in the argument names array. The getNonMatchingHeaders() method returns an Enumeration containing all the headers in this message with names that are *not* one of the strings in the argument names array. Again, the Enumeration contains Header objects:

```
public Enumeration getMatchingHeaders(String[] names)
    throws MessagingException
public Enumeration getNonMatchingHeaders(String[] names)
    throws MessagingException
```

Again, these methods are not genericized so you'll probably want to suppress generics warnings when invoking these methods.

You may recall that Example 7-1, HeaderClient, printed only a few prespecified headers, such as To: and From:. With the methods of the Part interface (that Message implements), it's easy to expand this to cover all headers in the message, whether known in advance or not. Example 7-4 demonstrates. This ability is important because email can contain arbitrary headers; it's not limited to just a few headers mentioned in the relevant RFCs. For instance, some graphical mail clients for X Windows use a completely non-standard X-Face: header, whose value is a 48-pixel by 48-pixel, black-and-white, uuencoded bitmap of the sender's countenance. Other clients use custom headers for purposes both more and less serious.

Example 7-4. A program to read mail headers

```java
import javax.mail.*;
import java.util.*;

public class AllHeaderClient {

  public static void main(String[] args) {

    if (args.length == 0) {
      System.err.println(
          "Usage: java AllHeaderClient protocol://username@host/foldername");
      return;
    }

    URLName server = new URLName(args[0]);

    try {
      Session session = Session.getInstance(new Properties(),
          new MailAuthenticator(server.getUsername()));

      // Connect to the server and open the folder
      Folder folder = session.getFolder(server);
      if (folder == null) {
        System.out.println("Folder " + server.getFile() + " not found.");
        System.exit(1);
      }
      folder.open(Folder.READ_ONLY);

      // Get the messages from the server
      Message[] messages = folder.getMessages();
      for (int i = 0; i < messages.length; i++) {
        System.out.println("------------ Message " + (i+1)
            + " ------------");
        // Here's the difference...
        @SuppressWarnings("unchecked")
        Enumeration<Header> headers = messages[i].getAllHeaders();
        while (headers.hasMoreElements()) {
          Header h = headers.nextElement();
          System.out.println(h.getName() + ": " + h.getValue());
        }
        System.out.println();
      }

      // Close the connection
      // but don't remove the messages from the server
      folder.close(false);
    } catch (MessagingException ex) {
      ex.printStackTrace();
    }

    // Since we may have brought up a GUI to authenticate,
    // we can't rely on returning from main() to exit
```

```
      System.exit(0);
  }
}
```

Here's a typical run:

```
% java AllHeaderClient pop3://eharold@utopia.poly.edu/INBOX
----------- Message 1 -----------
Received: (from eharold@localhost)
        by utopia.poly.edu (8.8.8/8.8.8) id QAA05728
        for eharold; Mon, 30 Nov 2009 16:14:29 -0500 (EST)
Date: Mon, 30 Nov 2009 16:14:29 -0500 (EST)
From: Elliotte Harold <eharold@utopia.poly.edu>
Message-Id: <200911302114.QAA05728@utopia.poly.edu>
To: eharold@utopia.poly.edu
Subject: test
Content-Type: text
X-UIDL: 87e3f1ba71738c8f772b15e3933241f0
Status: RO

----------- Message 2 -----------
Received: from russian.cloud9.net (russian.cloud9.net [168.100.1.4])
        by utopia.poly.edu (8.8.8/8.8.8) with ESMTP id OAA28428
        for <eharold@utopia.poly.edu>; Tue, 1 Dec 2009 14:05:06 -0500 (EST)
Received: from [168.100.203.234] (macfaq.dialup.cloud9.net [168.100.203.234])
        by russian.cloud9.net (Postfix) with ESMTP id 24B93764F8
        for <eharold@utopia.poly.edu>; Tue, 1 Dec 2009 14:02:50 -0500 (EST)
Mime-Version: 1.0
X-Sender: macfaq@mail.cloud9.net
Message-Id: <v04210100b46b1f97969d@[168.100.203.234]>
Date: Tue, 1 Dec 2009 13:55:40 -0500
To: eharold@utopia.poly.edu
From: Elliotte Rusty Harold <elharo@macfaq.com>
Subject: New system
Content-Type: text/plain; charset="us-ascii" ; format="flowed"
X-UIDL: 01fd5cbcf1768fc6c28f9c8f934534b5
Status: RO

----------- Message 3 -----------
Received: from russian.cloud9.net (russian.cloud9.net [168.100.1.4])
        by utopia.poly.edu (8.8.8/8.8.8) with ESMTP id HAA17345
        for <eharold@utopia.poly.edu>; Wed, 2 Dec 2009 07:55:04 -0500 (EST)
Received: from [168.100.203.234] (macfaq.dialup.cloud9.net [168.100.203.234])
        by russian.cloud9.net (Postfix) with ESMTP id C036A7630E
        for <eharold@utopia.poly.edu>; Wed, 2 Dec 2009 07:54:58 -0500 (EST)
Mime-Version: 1.0
X-Sender: elharo@luna.oit.unc.edu
Message-Id: <v04210100b46c0c686ecc@[168.100.203.234]>
Date: Wed, 2 Dec 2009 06:45:52 -0500
To: eharold@utopia.poly.edu
From: "Dr. Mickel" <Greatsmiles@mail.com>(by way of Elliotte Rusty Harold)
Subject: Breath RX Products now available Online!
Sender: elharo@ibiblio.org
```

```
Content-Type: text/plain; charset="us-ascii" ; format="flowed"
X-UIDL: 40fa8af2aca1a8c11994f4c56b792720
Status: RO
```

Content

Every part has content that can be represented as a sequence of bytes. For instance, in a part that's a simple email message, the content is the body of the message. However, in multipart messages, this content may itself contain other parts. The content of each of these parts can be represented as a sequence of bytes. Furthermore, this sequence of bytes may represent some more specific content type, such as a uuencoded GIF image or a Base64-encoded WAV audio clip.

Reading the contents of the part

The Part interface declares two methods for determining a part's MIME content type. The getContentType() method returns the MIME content type of the part as a string; for example: text/plain; charset="us-ascii"; format="flowed". It returns null if the content type can't be determined:

```
public String getContentType() throws MessagingException
```

The isMimeType() method returns true if this part has the specified MIME type and subtype. Additional parameters, such as charset, are ignored:

```
public boolean isMimeType(String mimeType) throws MessagingException
```

The Part interface also declares several methods that return the content as a variety of different Java objects, including InputStream, String, DataHandler, and more. The getInputStream() method returns an InputStream from which the part's content can be read:

```
public InputStream getInputStream()
    throws IOException, MessagingException
```

If the part's content has been encoded in some way—for example, Base64-encoded—then the InputStream reads the decoded content. The JavaMail API supports most common encodings.

Another possibility is to request a DataHandler for the content with the getDataHandler() method. The DataHandler class comes from the Java Activation Framework. It declares methods to help decide what to do with the content—for instance, by finding the right Java bean or helper application to display the content:

```
public javax.activation.DataHandler getDataHandler()
    throws MessagingException
```

A third possibility is to request the content as an unspecified Java object using the getContent() method:

```
public Object getContent() throws IOException, MessagingException
```

This is reminiscent of the getContent() method of java.net.URL. However, rather than relying on the poorly designed content handler mechanism, this getContent() method uses the Java Activation Framework, so the behavior is a little more clearly specified. Most of the time, if the content type is text/plain, a String will be returned. If the content type is multipart, then regardless of the subtype, a javax.mail.Multi part object is returned. If the content type is some other type that is recognized by the underlying DataHandler, an appropriate Java object is returned. Finally, if the type is unrecognized, an InputStream is returned.

Another way to read the contents of a part is by writing them onto an OutputStream using the writeTo() method. If necessary, it will encode the content using Base64, quoted-printable, or some other format as specified by the DataHandler:

```
public void writeTo(OutputStream out)
    throws IOException, MessagingException
```

In fact, this not only writes the content of this Part, it also writes the attributes and headers of the part. Example 6-1 used this to provide a simple way of getting an entire email message in one fell swoop. It's most convenient, though, when you want to send an entire message to an SMTP server in one method call.

If the part is not just a part, but specifically a MimeBodyPart (and most attachments in regular Internet email will be MimeBodyParts) then you can also use the saveFile() method to write the decoded contents of the part into a file:

```
public void saveFile(File file) throws IOException, MessagingException
public void saveFile(String file) throws IOException, MessagingException
```

Writing the contents of the part

When sending a message, you naturally must set the message's contents. Since email messages are text, the most straightforward way is just to provide the text of the part with setText():

```
public void setText(String text) throws MessagingException,
    IllegalWriteException, IllegalStateException
```

The setText() method sets the MIME type to text/plain. Other objects can be made into content as well, provided the part has a DataHandler that understands how to convert them to encoded text. This is done with the setContent() method:

```
public void setContent(Object o, String type) throws
    MessagingException, IllegalWriteException, IllegalStateException
```

Assuming you're sending Internet email, the concrete Part subclass will likely be Mime BodyPart, and in that case then you can also use the attachFile() method to encode the contents of a file into the message:

```
public void attachFile(File file) throws IOException, MessagingException
public void attachFile(String file) throws IOException, MessagingException
public void attachFile(File file, String contentType, String encoding)
    throws IOException, MessagingException
public void attachFile(String file, String contentType, String encoding)
    throws IOException, MessagingException
```

Finally, multiple parts can be added to a part by wrapping them in a `Multipart` object and passing that to `setContent()`:

```
public void setContent(Multipart mp) throws MessagingException,
    IllegalWriteException, IllegalStateException
```

In this case, the entire message typically has a content type such as `multipart/mixed`, `multipart/signed`, or `multipart/alternative`. The individual parts of the message are all enclosed in one envelope but each part of the message has its own content type, content encoding, and data. The multiple parts may be used to present different forms of the same document (e.g., HTML and plain-text mail), a document and metainformation about the document (e.g., a message and the MD5 digest of the message), or several different documents (e.g., a message and several attached files). The next section expands on this process.

Multipart Messages and File Attachments

The way all the different text and binary file types are encoded into raw text that can be passed through 7-bit email gateways is fairly ingenious and rather detailed. Fortunately, the JavaMail API shields you from those details, interesting as they are. To send a multipart message using the JavaMail API, all you have to do is add the parts to a `MimeMultipart` object, then pass that object to the `Message`'s `setContent()` method. To receive a multipart message, you simply process each of the parts individually.

Most of the methods for building and deconstructing multipart messages are in the abstract `javax.mail.Multipart` class:

```
public abstract class Multipart extends Object
```

However, since this class is abstract, you'll generally start with a javax.mail.internet.MimeMultipart object instead:

```
public class MimeMultipart extends Multipart
```

Each part you add to a `Multipart` is an instance of the abstract `javax.mail.Body` `Part` class that implements the `Part` interface of the last section:

```
public abstract class BodyPart extends Object implements Part
```

In Internet email, the concrete subclass of `BodyPart` you'll use is javax.mail.internet.MimeBodyPart:

```
public class MimeBodyPart extends BodyPart implements MimePart
```

Most of the methods you need in the `MimeBodyPart` and `BodyPart` classes are the ones you're already familiar with from the `Part` interface, methods such as `setContent()` and `setDataHandler()`. There are also three methods to read the contents of a `Multipart` object:

```
public String    getContentType()
public int        getCount() throws MessagingException
public BodyPart getBodyPart(int index)
  throws IndexOutOfBoundsException, MessagingException
```

The `getContentType()` method returns the MIME media type of the entire `Multipart`, which is typically something like `multipart/mixed` or `multipart/alternative`. This is not the same as the MIME types of the individual parts, which are something like `text/plain` or `image/gif`.

The `getCount()` method returns the number of parts in this `Multipart`. The `getBodyPart()` method returns a particular part. Parts are numbered starting at 0, like the components of an array. Example 7-5 is very similar to Example 7-4, `AllHeaderClient`. However, Example 7-5 adds the necessary code to handle the body of the message. If the message is a single-part message, it's simply printed on `System.out`; but if the message has multiple parts, each part is handled separately. If the part has a multipart content type itself, `processMultipart()` is called recursively. If the part has no filename, does not have the disposition `Part.ATTACHMENT`, and has MIME type `text/plain`, it's assumed to be an in-line message and is printed on `System.out`. Otherwise, it's assumed to be an attachment and is saved into an appropriate file. If necessary, the static `File.createTempFile()` method generates a reasonable name for the file.

Example 7-5. A mail client that handles multipart messages with attached files

```java
import java.util.*;
import java.io.*;
import javax.mail.*;

public class AllPartsClient {

  public static void main(String[] args) {

    if (args.length == 0) {
      System.err.println(
          "Usage: java AllPartsClient protocol://username@host:port/foldername");
      return;
    }
    URLName server = new URLName(args[0]);

    try {
      Session session = Session.getInstance(new Properties(),
          new MailAuthenticator(server.getUsername()));

      // Connect to the server and open the folder
```

```java
      Folder folder = session.getFolder(server);
      if (folder == null) {
        System.out.println("Folder " + server.getFile() + " not found.");
        System.exit(1);
      }
      folder.open(Folder.READ_ONLY);

      // Get the messages from the server
      Message[] messages = folder.getMessages();
      for (int i = 0; i < messages.length; i++) {
        System.out.println("------------ Message " + (i+1)
            + " ------------");

        // Print message headers
        @SuppressWarnings("unchecked")
        Enumeration<Header> headers = messages[i].getAllHeaders();
        while (headers.hasMoreElements()) {
          Header h = headers.nextElement();
          System.out.println(h.getName() + ": " + h.getValue());
        }
        System.out.println();

        // Enumerate parts
        Object body = messages[i].getContent();
        if (body instanceof Multipart) {
          processMultipart((Multipart) body);
        } else { // ordinary message
          processPart(messages[i]);
        }
        System.out.println();
      }

      // Close the connection
      // but don't remove the messages from the server
      folder.close(false);
    } catch (MessagingException| IOException ex) {
      ex.printStackTrace();
    }

    // Since we may have brought up a GUI to authenticate,
    // we can't rely on returning from main() to exit
    System.exit(0);
  }

  public static void processMultipart(Multipart mp)
      throws MessagingException {
    for (int i = 0; i < mp.getCount(); i++) {
      processPart(mp.getBodyPart(i));
    }
  }

  public static void processPart(Part p) {
```

```
    try {
      String fileName = p.getFileName();
      String disposition = p.getDisposition();
      String contentType = p.getContentType();
      if (contentType.toLowerCase().startsWith("multipart/")) {
        processMultipart((Multipart) p.getContent());
      } else if (fileName == null
          && (Part.ATTACHMENT.equalsIgnoreCase(disposition)
          || !contentType.equalsIgnoreCase("text/plain"))) {
        // pick a random file name.
        fileName = File.createTempFile("attachment", ".txt").getName();
      }

      if (fileName == null) { // likely inline
        p.writeTo(System.out);
      } else {
        File f = new File(fileName);
        // find a file that does not yet exist
        for (int i = 1; f.exists(); i++) {
          String newName = fileName + " " + i;
          f = new File(newName);
        }
        try (
          OutputStream out = new BufferedOutputStream(new FileOutputStream(f));
          InputStream in = new BufferedInputStream(p.getInputStream())) {
          // We can't just use p.writeTo() here because it doesn't
          // decode the attachment. Instead we copy the input stream
          // onto the output stream which does automatically decode
          // Base-64, quoted printable, and a variety of other formats.
          int b;
          while ((b = in.read()) != -1) out.write(b);
          out.flush();
        }
      }
    } catch (IOException| MessagingException ex) {
      ex.printStackTrace();
    }
  }
}
```

You can also get a part from a multipart message by passing an `OutputStream` to the part's `writeTo()` method:

```
public abstract void writeTo(OutputStream out)
    throws IOException, MessagingException
```

However, this differs from the approach taken in Example 7-4 in that it does not decode the part before writing it. It leaves whatever Base64, quoted-printable, or other encoding the sender applied to the attachment alone. Instead, it simply writes the raw data.

Attaching files (or other documents) to messages you send is more complicated. To attach a file to a message, you first have to wrap the data in a BodyPart object and add it to the Multipart using one of the two addBodyPart() methods:

```
public void addBodyPart(BodyPart part)
    throws IllegalWriteException, MessagingException
public void addBodyPart(BodyPart part, int index)
    throws IllegalWriteException, MessagingException
```

The first variant simply appends the part to the end of the message. The second variant adds the given part at the specified position. If the position is greater than the number of parts in the message, the part is simply added to the end. If it's added somewhere in the middle, this may cause the positions of other parts to change. If the message can't be changed, an IllegalWriteException is thrown.

The tricky part is creating the BodyPart object. You first need to guess a reasonable MIME content type for the file (text/plain and application/octet-stream are the most common types). Next, read the file and convert it into some class of Java object. Then install a javax.activation.DataHandler class that knows how to convert your data class according to your chosen MIME type. Once you've done all this, you can create a new MimeBodyPart object and use the various methods of the Part interface to set attributes such as the filename and the content disposition.

There are also two removeBodyPart() methods that delete a specified part from the message, although these aren't as commonly used:

```
public boolean removeBodyPart(BodyPart part)
    throws IllegalWriteException, MessagingException
public void removeBodyPart(int index)
    throws IndexOutOfBoundsException, MessagingException
```

If the message can't be changed, an IllegalWriteException is thrown. If the specified index doesn't identify a part, an IndexOutOfBoundsException is thrown. If the specified part isn't present in the message, a MessagingException is thrown.

MIME Messages

MIME was designed mainly for Internet email and specifically organized to be backward-compatible with existing protocols and software. Therefore, a typical Internet email message is in fact a MIME message. The only concrete subclass of Message in the JavaMail API is javax.mail.internet.MimeMessage :

```
public class MimeMessage extends Message implements MimePart
```

This class declares almost 70 public and protected methods. However, almost all of these either override methods from the Message superclass or implement methods declared by the `Part` interface. The only new methods are declared in the `MimePart` interface, a subinterface of `Part`:

```
public interface MimePart extends Part
```

Most of these methods are very similar to methods in `Part` or `Message`. However, they have features that are unlikely to be found in non-MIME messages. For instance, a MIME part may have an MD5 digest, which would be encoded as an extra header inside the part. Thus, the `MimePart` interface declares and the `MimeMessage` class implements two methods to get and set this digest:

```
public String getContentMD5() throws MessagingException
public void    setContentMD5(String md5) throws MessagingException,
    IllegalWriteException, IllegalStateException
```

The `addHeaderLine()` method adds a string of text to the header of the message. It's up to you to make sure that this string will actually make sense in the header:

```
public void addHeaderLine(String line) throws
    MessagingException, IllegalWriteException, IllegalStateException
```

The `getHeader()` method returns the value of every header in the message with the given name. If there are multiple headers with this name, the string separates the values of the different headers with the specified `delimiter` string:

```
public String getHeader(String name, String delimiter)
    throws MessagingException
```

The `getAllHeaderLines()` method returns a `java.util.Enumeration` containing every header in the message. The `Enumeration` contains `String` objects, one per header. Each `String` contains the full name and value; for example, "Subject: Re: Java 5 support". It is not divided into a separate name and value:

```
public Enumeration getAllHeaderLines() throws MessagingException
```

The `getMatchingHeaderLines()` method returns all header lines with names given in the `names` argument array. The `getNonMatchingHeaderLines()` method does the reverse; it returns the header lines with a name not mentioned in the `names` argument:

```
public Enumeration getMatchingHeaderLines(String[] names)
    throws MessagingException
public Enumeration getNonMatchingHeaderLines(String[] names)
    throws MessagingException
```

The `getEncoding()` method returns the encoding of this MIME part as a `String` as given by the Content-transfer-encoding: header. The typical encoding for a plain-text email is seven-bit or perhaps eight-bit or quoted-printable. The typical encoding for a file attachment is Base64:

```
public String getEncoding() throws MessagingException
```

The getContentID() method returns a string that uniquely identifies this part as given by the part's Content-ID: field. A typical ID might look like *<Pine.LNX. 4.10.9912290930220.8058@akbar.nevex.com>*. It returns null if the part doesn't have a content ID:

```
public String getContentID() throws MessagingException
    IllegalWriteException, IllegalStateException
```

The getContentLanguage() method returns the value of the Content-language: header. This is a comma-separated list of two (or more) letter abbreviations for languages, as defined by RFC 1766. For example, English is "en" and French is "fr". It returns null if the part doesn't have a Content-language: header.

```
public String[] getContentLanguage() throws MessagingException
```

There's also a setContentLanguage() method that you might use when sending a message:

```
public void setContentLanguage(String[] languages) throws
    MessagingException, IllegalWriteException, IllegalStateException
```

Finally, the two setText() methods set the content of the part with the MIME type text/plain. The second setText() method also lets you specify the character set—for example, us-ascii or ISO 8859-1:

```
public void setText(String text) throws MessagingException
public void setText(String text, String charset)
    throws MessagingException
public void setText(String text, String charset, String subtype)
    throws MessagingException
```

In practice, a number of mail systems and libraries, especially Japanese ones, do not correctly implement every detail of the relevant specifications. Consequently the Java-Mail API recognizes a number of system properties that control exactly how strictly various rules are followed. Table 7-1 lists the various system properties that control MIME parsing. With a couple of exceptions the default values provide standards conformant behavior, and changing these breaks conformance to work better with some mail agents encountered in the wild.

Table 7-1. MIME System Properties

Property	Default Value	Purpose
mail.mime.decodetext.strict	true	Do not decode messages that do not conform to RFC 2047
mail.mime.encodeeol.strict	false	Interpret a carriage return linefeed pair as a line break when they occur in a mail message part that does not have MIME media type of text.
mail.mime.address.strict	true	Throw an `AddressException` when parsing an email address that is not spec conformant; e.g. usernames without an "@domain" part.
mail.mime.charset	file.encoding	The character set to use when reading messages that don't specify their own character set.
mail.mime.decodefilename	false	Use `MimeUtility.decodeText()` to decode non-ASCII characters in the filename.
mail.mime.encodefilename	false	Use `MimeUtility.encodeText()` to encode non-ASCII characters in the filename.
mail.mime.decodeparameters	false	Decode non-ASCII parameters e.g., in a Content-Type header, as specified by RFC 2231.
mail.mime.encodeparameters	false	Encode non-ASCII parameters, e.g., in a Content-Type header, as specified by RFC 2231.
mail.mime.multipart.ignoremissingendboundary	true	Throw a `MessagingException` when a message is missing the final end boundary line
mail.mime.multipart.ignoremissingboundaryparameter	true	Throw a `MessagingException` when a Content-Type header does not have a boundary parameter.
mail.mime.base64.ignoreerrors	false	The BASE64 decoder returns EOF and skips remaining data on encountering an encoding error.
mail.mime.foldtext	true	Break header fields into 76 character lines.
mail.mime.setcontenttypefilename	true	`setFileName()` also sets the name parameter in the Content-Type header.
mail.mime.setdefaulttextcharset	true	Add missing charset parameters.
mail.mime.parameters.strict	true	Header fields such as Content-Type are not allowed to contain whitespace and other special characters unless quoted.
mail.mime.windowsfilenames	false	Workaround bugs in the Content-Disposition header of messages created by Internet Explorer 6.
mail.mime.ignoreunknownencoding	false	Treat unknown values in the Content-Transfer-Encoding header as "8bit."
mail.mime.uudecode.ignoreerrors	false	Ignore errors in the encoded format of a uuencoded document.
mail.mime.uudecode.ignoremissingbeginend	false	Ignore a missing "begin" or "end" line in a uuencoded document.

Property	Default Value	Purpose
mail.mime.multipart.allowempty	false	Do not throw a `MessagingException` when writing or parsing a multipart message without a body part.
mail.mime.multipart.ignoreexistingboundaryparameter	false	Workaround for broken anti-virus products that rewrite messages.
mail.mime.multipart.ignorewhitespacelines	false	Allow a line containing only white space but not empty to separate the header from the body.
mail.mime.ignoremultipartencoding	true	Use Content-Transfer-Encoding for multipart content too.
mail.mime.allowencodedmessages	false	Use Content-Transfer-Encoding for message/* content too to work around Outlook bugs.

CHAPTER 8

Folders

So far, we've worked mostly with the INBOX folder. This is the default folder in which most mail resides until the user filters or saves it into some other folder. On some systems, it may actually reside in a file called INBOX. On other systems, it may be called something different. Nonetheless, you can always access it from the JavaMail API using the name INBOX.

Most mail programs allow you to organize your messages into different folders. These folders are hierarchical; that is, a folder may contain another folder. In particular, in the IMAP protocol, servers store the messages in different folders from which clients retrieve and manipulate the messages as necessary. POP servers, by contrast, generally send all the messages to the user when the user connects and rely on the client to store and manage them. The primary advantage of the IMAP approach over POP is that it allows users to easily access their entire email archives from multiple client machines.

The JavaMail API represents IMAP-like folders as instances of the abstract Folder class:

```
public abstract class Folder extends Object
```

This class declares methods for requesting named folders from servers, deleting messages from folders, searching for particular messages in folders, listing the messages in a folder, and so forth. Most of these methods are declared abstract. When you ask a session, a store, or a folder to give you one of the folders it contains, it will give you an instance of a concrete subclass appropriate for the protocol in use: IMAP, POP, mbox, or whatever. The reference implementation of the JavaMail API knows how to do these operations only for IMAP servers. However, some third-party implementations provide these operations in local mailbox folders stored on the client's filesystem as well.

Opening Folders

You cannot create folders directly. The only constructor is protected. Instead, you get a Folder from a Session, a Store, or another Folder like this:

```
Folder outbox = container.getFolder("sent-mail");
```

There are actually three getFolder() methods, one each in the Session, Store, and Folder classes. They all have the same signature and behave similarly:

```
public abstract Folder getFolder(String name) throws MessagingException
```

These methods share an annoying idiosyncrasy with the File class. Getting a Folder object doesn't imply that the named Folder actually exists on the server. To tell whether the folder is really present, you have to test for it with the exists() method:

```
public boolean exists() throws MessagingException
```

When you first get a folder, it's closed. Before you can read the messages it contains, you have to open the folder using the open() method:

```
public abstract void open(int mode)
    throws FolderNotFoundException, MessagingException
```

The mode argument should be one of the two named constants, Folder.READ_ONLY or Folder.READ_WRITE. Some but not all implementations allow you to open multiple connections to one real folder using multiple Folder objects.

Some operations discussed in this section, such as searching or retrieving messages from a folder, can only be performed on an open folder. Others, such as deleting or changing the name of a folder, can only be done to a closed folder. The isOpen() method returns true if the folder is open, false if it's closed:

```
public abstract boolean isOpen()
```

Generally, trying to do something with a closed folder that requires the folder to be open or vice versa will throw a java.lang.IllegalStateException. This is a runtime exception, so it doesn't need to be explicitly caught or declared.

When you're done with a folder, close it using the close() method:

```
public abstract void close(boolean expunge)
    throws FolderNotFoundException, MessagingException
```

If the expunge argument is true, any deleted messages in the folder are deleted from the actual file on the server. Otherwise, they're simply marked as deleted, but the messages can still be undeleted.

Folder does not implement AutoCloseable so even in Java 7 you may want to use the dispose pattern to close a folder in a finally block. You'll want to check both that the folder is not null and that it's open.

```
Folder folder = null;
try {
  // Connect to the server and open the folder
  folder = session.getFolder(server);
  // work with the folder...
} catch (MessagingException | IOException ex) {
  ex.printStackTrace();
} finally {
  // Close the connection
  // but don't remove the messages from the server
  if (folder != null && folder.isOpen()) {
    try {
      folder.close(false);
    } catch (MessagingException e) {
      // ignore;
    }
  }
}
```

Basic Folder Info

The Folder class has eight methods that return basic information about a folder:

```
public abstract String  getName()
public abstract String  getFullName()
public URLName          getURLName() throws MessagingException
public abstract Folder  getParent() throws MessagingException
public abstract int     getType() throws MessagingException
public int              getMode() throws IllegalStateException
public Store            getStore()
public abstract char    getSeparator()
    throws FolderNotFoundException, MessagingException
```

The getName() method returns the name of the folder, such as "Reader Mail", whereas the getFullName() method returns the complete hierarchical name from the root, such as "books/JNP4E/Reader Mail". In this example, the slash character is the separator between nested folders. The separator can vary from implementation to implementation, but the getSeparator() method always tells you what it is.

The getURLName() method includes the server; for instance, "imap:// elharo@mail.ibiblio.org/books/JNP4E/Reader%20Mail".

The getParent() method returns the name of the folder that contains this folder; e.g., "JNP4E" for the previous Reader Mail example.

The getType() method returns an int indicating whether the folder can contain messages and/or other folders. If it can contain messages but not folders, getType() returns the named constant Folder.HOLDS_MESSAGES. If it can contain folders but not messages, getType() returns the named constant Folder.HOLDS_FOLDERS. If it can contain both folders and messages, `getType()` returns the bitwise union `Folder.HOLDS_FOLDERS | Folder.HOLDS_MESSAGES`.

The `getMode()` method tells you whether a folder allows writing. It returns one of the two named constants (`Folder.READ_ONLY` or `Folder.READ_WRITE`) or -1 if the mode is unknown. Finally, the `getStore()` method returns the `Store` object from which this folder was retrieved.

Managing Folders

The `create()` method creates a new folder in this folder's `Store`:

```
public abstract boolean create(int type) throws MessagingException
```

The type of the folder should be one of the named constants `Folder.HOLDS_MESSAGES` or `Folder.HOLDS_FOLDERS`, depending on whether it will hold other folders or messages. It returns `true` if the creation succeeded, `false` if it didn't.

The `delete()` method deletes this folder, but only if the folder is closed. Otherwise, it throws an `IllegalStateException`:

```
public abstract boolean delete(boolean recurse) throws
    IllegalStateException, FolderNotFoundException, MessagingException
```

If there are messages in this folder, they are deleted along with the folder. If the folder contains subfolders, the subfolders are deleted if the `recurse` argument is `true`. If the `recurse` argument is not `true`, the folder will only be deleted if it does not contain any subfolders. If it does contain subfolders, the delete fails. If the folder does contain subfolders and also contains messages, it's implementation-dependent whether the messages will be deleted even though the folder itself isn't. If the delete succeeds, the method returns `true`; otherwise, it returns `false`.

The `renameTo()` method changes the name of this folder. A folder must be closed to be renamed. Otherwise, an `IllegalStateException` is thrown. This method returns `true` if the folder is successfully renamed, `false` if it isn't:

```
public abstract boolean renameTo(Folder f) throws
    IllegalStateException, FolderNotFoundException, MessagingException
```

Managing Messages in Folders

On occasion, you may find a need to put a message in a folder. For instance, after sending a message, a mail program may place it in a "Sent" folder. There's only one method to do this, `appendMessages()`:

```
public abstract void appendMessages(Message[] messages)
    throws FolderNotFoundException, MessagingException
```

As the name implies, the messages in the array are placed at the end of this folder.

The `copyMessages()` method copies messages from this folder into a specified folder given as an argument:

```
public void copyMessages(Message[] messages, Folder destination) throws
    IllegalStateException, FolderNotFoundException, MessagingException
```

The copied messages are appended to the destination folder. They are not removed from the source folder. To move a message, you have to copy it from the source to the destination, delete it from the source folder, and finally expunge the source folder.

To delete a message from a folder, set its `Flags.Flag.DELETED` flag to `true`. To physically remove deleted messages from a folder, you have to call its `expunge()` method:

```
public abstract Message[] expunge() throws MessagingException,
    IllegalStateException, FolderNotFoundException
```

After a message has been expunged, there may still be `Message` objects that refer to it. In this case, almost any method call on such an object, except `isExpunged()` and `get MessageNumber()`, will throw an exception.

Subscriptions

Some implementations allow you to subscribe to particular folders. This would be most appropriate for an NNTP provider, where a typical server offers thousands of newsgroups, but the typical user will want to retrieve messages from a few dozen of these, at most. Each newsgroup would be represented as a `Folder` object. A subscription to the newsgroup's `Folder` indicates that the user wants to retrieve messages from that newsgroup:

```
public boolean isSubscribed()
public void    setSubscribed(boolean subscribe)
    throws FolderNotFoundException, MethodNotSupportedException,
    MessagingException
```

Subscriptions are sometimes also used in IMAP to specify a subset of a user's folders that need to be cached locally or prefetched.

If a provider doesn't support subscription, `setSubscribed()` throws a `MethodNotSup portedException` and `isSubscribed()` returns `false`.

Listing the Contents of a Folder

There are four methods to list the folders that a folder contains:

```
public Folder[] list()
    throws FolderNotFoundException, MessagingException
public Folder[] listSubscribed()
```

```
      throws FolderNotFoundException, MessagingException
public abstract Folder[] list(String pattern)
      throws FolderNotFoundException, MessagingException
public Folder[] listSubscribed(String pattern)
      throws FolderNotFoundException, MessagingException
```

The first method returns an array listing the folders that this folder contains. The second method returns an array listing all the subscribed folders that this folder contains.

The third and fourth methods repeat these first two, except they allow you to specify a pattern. Only folders whose full names match the pattern will be in the returned array. The pattern is a string giving the name of the folders that match. However, the string can contain the % character, which is a wildcard that matches any sequence of characters not including the hierarchy separator, and *, which matches any sequence of characters including the hierarchy separator.

Checking for Mail

The getMessageCount() method returns the number of messages in this folder:

```
public abstract int getMessageCount()
      throws FolderNotFoundException, MessagingException
```

This method can be invoked on an open or closed folder. However, in the case of a closed folder, this method may (or may not) return -1 to indicate that the exact number of messages isn't easily available.

The hasNewMessages() method returns true if new messages have been added to the folder since it was last opened (not since the last time you checked!):

```
public abstract boolean hasNewMessages()
      throws FolderNotFoundException, MessagingException
```

The getNewMessageCount() method uses a slightly different approach for determining how many new messages there are. It checks the number of messages in the folder whose RECENT flag is set:

```
public int getNewMessageCount()
      throws FolderNotFoundException, MessagingException
```

Unlike hasNewMessages(), getNewMessageCount() can be invoked on either an open or a closed folder. However, in the case of a closed folder, getNewMessageCount() may return -1 to indicate that the real answer would be too expensive to obtain.

The getUnreadMessageCount() method is similar but returns the number of messages in the folder that do not have a SEEN flag set:

```
public int getUnreadMessageCount()
      throws FolderNotFoundException, MessagingException
```

Like `getNewMessageCount()`, `getUnreadMessageCount()` can be invoked on either an open or a closed folder. However, in the case of a closed folder, it may return -1 to indicate that the real answer would be too expensive to obtain.

Getting Messages from Folders

The `Folder` class provides four methods for retrieving messages from open folders:

```
public abstract Message getMessage(int messageNumber) throws
    IndexOutOfBoundsException, FolderNotFoundException,
    IllegalStateException, MessagingException
public Message[] getMessages() throws FolderNotFoundException,
    IllegalStateException, MessagingException
public Message[] getMessages(int start, int end) throws
    IndexOutOfBoundsException, FolderNotFoundException,
    IllegalStateException, MessagingException
public Message[] getMessages(int[] messageNumbers) throws
    IndexOutOfBoundsException, FolderNotFoundException,
    IllegalStateException, MessagingException
```

The `getMessage()` method returns the nth message in the folder. The first message in the folder is number 1 (not 0). Message numbers may change when messages are expunged from the folder. An `IndexOutOfBoundsException` is thrown if you ask for message n and there are $n - 1$ or fewer messages in the folder.

The first `getMessages()` method returns an array of `Message` objects representing all the messages in this folder. The second `getMessages()` method returns an array of `Message` objects from the folder, beginning with `start` and finishing with `end`, inclusive. The third `getMessages()` method returns an array containing only those messages specifically identified by number in the `messageNumbers` array.

All four of these methods only create the `Message` objects and fill in the minimal number of fields in those objects. The actual text and other content of the message is fetched from the server when the `Message`'s methods that use those things are invoked. This means, for example, that you can't get all the messages from the server, then get on an airplane and work with them offline. There is, however, a `fetch()` method, which fills in certain parts of the `Message` objects with actual data from the server:

```
public void fetch(Message[] messages, FetchProfile fp)
    throws IllegalStateException, MessagingException
```

The `messages` argument is an array containing the `Message` objects to be prefetched. The `FetchProfile` argument specifies which headers in the messages to prefetch. However, this is still just a suggestion. Implementations are free to ignore this request and fetch the message content only when it's actually needed.

You can request prefetching of individual headers such as Subject: by name. You can also request prefetching of three predefined blocks of information: the envelope (essentially the subject and addressees of the message), the flags of the message, or the content info of the messages. The three groups you can ask for are given as constant `FetchProfile.Item` objects. They are `FetchProfile.Item.ENVELOPE`, `FetchPro file.Item.FLAGS`, and `FetchProfile.Item.CONTENT_INFO`.

The `FetchProfile` class has a simple noargs constructor as well as methods for constructing a new profile, adding particular items and headers to the profile, and testing whether a particular item is part of a particular profile:

```
public FetchProfile()
public void add(FetchProfile.Item item)
public void add(String headerName)
public boolean contains(FetchProfile.Item item)
public boolean contains(String headerName)
public FetchProfile.Item[] getItems()
public String[] getHeaderNames()
```

For example, suppose you wanted to download just the subjects, the To: addresses, and the content information of a block of messages. Fetch them like this:

```
Message[] messages = folder.getMessages();
FetchProfile fp = new FetchProfile();
fp.add(FetchProfile.Item.CONTENT_INFO);
fp.add("Subject");
fp.add("To");
folder.fetch(messages, fp);
```

Searching Folders

If the server supports searching (as many IMAP servers do and most POP servers don't), it's easy to search a folder for the messages meeting certain criteria. The criteria are encoded in `SearchTerm` objects:

```
public abstract class SearchTerm extends Object
```

The `SearchTerm` class is abstract, but the JavaMail API provides many subclasses for performing common searches:

```
public abstract class    AddressTerm        extends SearchTerm
public abstract class    FlagTerm           extends SearchTerm
public abstract class    StringTerm         extends SearchTerm
public final    class    FromTerm           extends AddressTerm
public final    class    FromStringTerm     extends AddressStringTerm
public final    class    RecipientTerm      extends AddressTerm
public final    class    AddressStringTerm  extends StringTerm
public final    class    BodyTerm           extends StringTerm
public final    class    HeaderTerm         extends StringTerm
public final    class    MessageIDTerm      extends StringTerm
public final    class    SubjectTerm        extends StringTerm
public abstract class    DateTerm           extends ComparisonTerm
```

```
public final    class    ReceivedDateTerm  extends DateTerm
public final    class    SentDateTerm      extends DateTerm
```

It also provides several classes for combining searches:

```
public final    class AndTerm         extends SearchTerm
public abstract class ComparisonTerm  extends SearchTerm
public final    class NotTerm         extends SearchTerm
public final    class OrTerm          extends SearchTerm
```

Set up a `SearchTerm` matching your desired parameters and pass it to one of these two search() methods in the `Folder` class:

```
public Message[] search(SearchTerm term) throws SearchException,
    FolderNotFoundException, IllegalStateException, MessagingException
public Message[] search(SearchTerm term, Message[] messages)
    throws SearchException, FolderNotFoundException,
    IllegalStateException, MessagingException
```

A `SearchException` indicates that the search term is more complicated than the implementation can handle.

For example, this search term seeks out all messages from *billg@microsoft.com*:

```
Address billg  = new InternetAddress("billg@microsoft.com");
SearchTerm term = new FromTerm(billg);
```

This search term looks for all messages from *billg@microsoft.com* in 2012 or later:

```
Address billg = new InternetAddress("billg@microsoft.com");
SearchTerm term1 = new FromTerm(billg);
Calendar calendar = Calendar.getInstance();
calendar.set(2012, 0, 1);
Date date = calendar.getTime();
SearchTerm term2 = new SentDateTerm(ComparisonTerm.GE, date);
SearchTerm term  = new AndTerm(term1, term2);
```

Example 8-1 is a simple variation of the `MailClient` program in Example 6-1. It allows the user to list email addresses on the command line after the initial URL, like this:

```
% java SearchClient imap://elharo@mail.ibiblio.org/INBOX
    willis@nvx.com billg@microsoft.com
```

Only messages from the specified users will be returned. However, if no email addresses are given, all messages will be returned.

Example 8-1. A mail client that searches by From: address

```
import javax.mail.*;
import javax.mail.search.*;
import javax.mail.internet.*;
import java.util.*;
import java.io.*;

public class SearchClient {
```

```java
public static void main(String[] args) {

  if (args.length == 0) {
    System.err.println(
        "Usage: java SearchClient protocol://username@host/foldername");
    return;
  }

  URLName server = new URLName(args[0]);
  Folder folder = null;
  try {
    Session session = Session.getInstance(new Properties(),
        new MailAuthenticator(server.getUsername()));

    // Connect to the server and open the folder
    folder = session.getFolder(server);
    if (folder == null) {
      System.out.println("Folder " + server.getFile() + " not found.");
      System.exit(1);
    }
    folder.open(Folder.READ_ONLY);

    SearchTerm term = null;
    if (args.length > 1) {
      SearchTerm[] terms = new SearchTerm[args.length-1];
      for (int i = 1; i < args.length; i++) {
        terms[i-1] = new FromTerm(new InternetAddress(args[i]));
      }
      if (terms.length > 1) term = new OrTerm(terms);
      else term = terms[0];
    }

    // Get the messages from the server
    Message[] messages;
    if (term == null)  {
      messages = folder.getMessages();
    } else {
      messages = folder.search(term);
    }
    for (int i = 0; i < messages.length; i++) {
      System.out.println("------------ Message " + (i+1)
          + " ------------");

      // Print message headers
      @SuppressWarnings("unchecked")
      Enumeration<Header> headers = messages[i].getAllHeaders();
      while (headers.hasMoreElements()) {
        Header h = headers.nextElement();
        System.out.println(h.getName() + ": " + h.getValue());
      }
      System.out.println();
```

```java
      // Enumerate parts
      Object body = messages[i].getContent();
      if (body instanceof Multipart) {
        processMultipart((Multipart) body);
      } else { // ordinary message
        processPart(messages[i]);
      }

      System.out.println();
    }
  } catch (MessagingException | IOException ex) {
    ex.printStackTrace();
  } finally {
    // Close the connection
    // but don't remove the messages from the server
    if (folder != null && folder.isOpen())
      try {
        folder.close(false);
      } catch (MessagingException e) {
        // ignore;
      }
  }

  // Since we may have brought up a GUI to authenticate,
  // we can't rely on returning from main() to exit
  System.exit(0);
}

public static void processMultipart(Multipart mp)
    throws MessagingException {
  for (int i = 0; i < mp.getCount(); i++) {
    processPart(mp.getBodyPart(i));
  }
}

public static void processPart(Part p) {
  try {
    // I'd prefer to test the Content-Disposition header here.
    // However, too many common email clients don't use it.
    String fileName = p.getFileName();
    if (fileName == null) { // likely inline
      p.writeTo(System.out);
    } else if (fileName != null) {
      File f = new File(fileName);
      // find a version that does not yet exist
      for (int i = 1; f.exists(); i++) {
        String newName = fileName + " " + i;
        f = new File(newName);
      }

      try (FileOutputStream out = new FileOutputStream(f);
          InputStream in = new BufferedInputStream(p.getInputStream())) {
```

```
        // We can't just use p.writeTo() here because it doesn't
        // decode the attachment. Instead we copy the input stream
        // onto the output stream which does automatically decode
        // Base-64, quoted printable, and a variety of other formats.
        int b;
        while ((b = in.read()) != -1) out.write(b);
        out.flush();
      }
    }
  } catch (MessagingException | IOException ex) {
    ex.printStackTrace();
  }
 }
}
```

Flags

It's sometimes useful to change the flags for an entire group of messages at once. The
Folder class has three methods for doing this:

```
public void setFlags(Message[] messages, Flags flag, boolean value)
    throws IllegalStateException, MessagingException
public void setFlags(int start, int end, Flags flag, boolean value)
    throws IllegalStateException, MessagingException
public void setFlags(int[] messageNumbers, Flags flag, boolean value)
    throws IndexOutOfBoundsException, IllegalStateException,
    MessagingException
```

Ultimately, these are just conveniences. There's nothing you can do with these methods
that you can't do by setting the flags on each message individually with the set
Flags() method of the Message class. In fact, the default implementation simply invokes
that method on each message in the specified block of messages.

The Folder class also has a getPermanentFlags() method to return the flags that this
folder supports for all messages. This includes all the flags except the user-defined flags,
which are applied only to particular messages that the user has flagged. For instance,
not all folder implementations track whether messages have been answered:

```
public abstract Flags getPermanentFlags()
```

CHAPTER 9

Event Handling

Many email programs can periodically check for incoming email in the background. One way to structure an email program is as a series of responses to unpredictable events. This is much like programming for a graphical user interface, and indeed the JavaMail API uses the same Observer pattern to handle mail events that JavaBeans and Swing use to handle GUI events.

The JavaMail API defines six different kinds of mail events, all in the `javax.mail.event` package. They are all subclasses of `MailEvent`:

```
public abstract class MailEvent extends EventObject
```

The six concrete kinds of mail events are:

ConnectionEvent

> A `Folder`, `Store`, or `Transport` has been opened, closed, or disconnected.

FolderEvent

> A `Folder` has been created, deleted, or renamed.

MessageChangedEvent

> The message's envelope or flags have changed.

MessageCountEvent

> A message was added to or deleted from a `Folder`.

StoreEvent

> A notification or alert from a `Store`.

TransportEvent

> A notification from a `Transport` that a message was delivered, partially delivered, or failed to be delivered.

There are six listener interfaces corresponding to the six kinds of events:

```
public interface ConnectionListener       extends EventListener
public interface FolderListener           extends EventListener
public interface MessageChangedListener   extends EventListener
public interface MessageCountListener     extends EventListener
public interface StoreListener            extends EventListener
public interface TransportListener        extends EventListener
```

Each of these interfaces declares one or more methods that must be provided by implementing classes. For example, the ConnectionListener class declares these three methods:

```
public void opened(ConnectionEvent event)
public void disconnected(ConnectionEvent event)
public void closed(ConnectionEvent event)
```

The FolderListener interface declares these three methods:

```
public void folderCreated(FolderEvent event)
public void folderDeleted(FolderEvent event)
public void folderRenamed(FolderEvent event)
```

Four of these events can be fired by folders. Consequently, there are 8 addXXXListener() and removeXXXListener() methods in the Folder class:

```
public void addConnectionListener(ConnectionListener listener)
public void removeConnectionListener(ConnectionListener listener)
public void addFolderListener(FolderListener listener)
public void removeFolderListener(FolderListener listener)
public void addMessageCountListener(MessageCountListener listener)
public void removeMessageCountListener(MessageCountListener listener)
public void addMessageChangedListener(MessageChangedListener listener)
public void removeMessageChangedListener(MessageChangedListener listener)
```

The addXXXListener() methods add an implementation of the particular interface to the list of listeners. The removeXXXListener() methods remove an implementation from that list. All of this works exactly as it does in JavaBeans and Swing, just with different events.

For example, suppose you want to be notified every time a new email message arrives. First you implement the MessageCountListener interface with a class that responds to message added events as shown in Example 9-1.

Example 9-1. Message Notifier

```
import javax.mail.*;
import javax.mail.event.*;

public class MessageArrival implements MessageCountListener {

  @Override
  public void messagesAdded(MessageCountEvent event) {
    Message[] newMessages = event.getMessages();
    for (Message message : newMessages) {
```

```
      try {
        System.out.println(message.getSubject());
      } catch (MessagingException e) {
        System.out.println("New message arrived!");
      }
    }
  }
}

  @Override
  public void messagesRemoved(MessageCountEvent event) {
    // ignore
  }

}
```

This class notifies the user by printing a message on the console. Of course, you could pop up an alert in a GUI, ring a bell, or use any other technique you like.

Next you install this listener on the folder you wish to monitor as shown in Example 9-2.

Example 9-2. Mailbox Monitor

```
import java.util.*;
import javax.mail.*;
import javax.mail.event.*;

import com.sun.mail.imap.IMAPStore;

public class GMailMonitor {

  public static void main(String[] args) throws InterruptedException {
    String username = args[0];
    String password = args[1];
    try {
      Session session = Session.getInstance(new Properties());
      final IMAPStore store = (IMAPStore) session.getStore("imaps");
      store.connect("imap.gmail.com", username + "@gmail.com", password);

      final Folder inbox = store.getFolder("INBOX");
      if (inbox == null) {
        System.out.println("No INBOX");
        System.exit(1);
      }
      inbox.open(Folder.READ_ONLY);
      MessageCountListener countListener = new MessageArrival();
      inbox.addMessageCountListener(countListener);

      Runnable r = new Runnable() {
        @Override
        public void run() {
          while (true) {
            try {
              System.out.println(inbox.getMessageCount());
```

```
                System.out.println("Idling");
                store.idle();
              } catch (MessagingException ex) {
                ex.printStackTrace();
                return;
              }
            }
          }
        };
        Thread t = new Thread(r);
        t.start();
      } catch (MessagingException ex) {
        ex.printStackTrace();
      }
    }
  }
}
```

Note that in this case it's not enough to simply install a listener. The server won't push information to the client. The client has to contact the server. To make this happen, Example 9-2 spawns a separate thread that periodically sends idle() commands to the IMAP server. The server can respond to one of these when it has something to say. Otherwise the connection is just held open indefinitely.

Now every time a message arrives in the INBOX, its subject will be logged to System.out.

Epilogue: Email Past and Future

I'm dating myself here, but I remember a time when AOL was obviously going to replace email (or at least that's what the pundits and day traders told us). Standard Internet email was clearly too anarchic, uncontrolled, and uncommercial to be suitable for real business. Now that email was escaping the ivory towers of academia, it had to be owned and managed by a corporation. That…didn't happen.

A few years later, MySpace was obviously going to replace email. Email was only used by old fogies like myself. Anyone under 18 didn't send or read email; and as they grew up, graduated from college, and joined the work force, email was going to fade away much like Usenet news before it. That also…didn't happen.

MySpace sold itself to Rupert Murdoch and promptly imploded. The teenagers who made MySpace the new hotness rapidly defected to upstart Facebook. And for a few years the same talking heads who had told us AOL and MySpace were going to replace email were now saying that Facebook was going to replace email. Email had become choked with spam and thus useless. Clearly Facebook was the wave of the future. By this point the articles and blog posts were beginning to sound a little familiar, as if someone had just done s/MySpace/Facebook and rerun the same pieces. In any case, once again that…didn't happen.

That's only a brief selection of "email killers" that have been sold to us over the last decade and a half. MSN, Twitter, text messages, YouTube, Skype, and more have all been heralded as email replacements. I'd lay good money that email will outlast all of them. By this point it should be obvious that email is here to stay. While SMTP, POP, IMAP, DNS, MX records, and even TCP itself are imperfect, they hit a real sweet spot. They are more than good enough to solve the fundamental problem of enabling people to communicate asynchronously with written messages without being locked into any one network or provider.

The protocols have evolved over time. Security has become vastly more important. More connections are encrypted than ever before (and even more should be). Authentication and authorization are enforced at most ingress points to the network which alleviates some of the more casual spamming and forgery problems. Unicode has mostly replaced ASCII and other national character sets. Attachments, MIME, and multipart messages were added before some of the people reading this book were born. More changes are likely in the future.

Nonetheless, the basic architecture of email communication has remained remarkably consistent for more than 30 years and seems likely to continue for at least another 30. People need email, and they need to send it to other people who don't use the same ISP or service they do. No single service, no single website, can hope to replace it.

As important as HTTP has become, it is not the only protocol needed on today's or tomorrow's Internet. SMTP is just as important and POP and IMAP only slightly less so. Programs that push information to people instead of waiting for people to request it need email. Such programs written in Java need the JavaMail API.

About the Author

Elliotte Rusty Harold is originally from New Orleans, to which he returns periodically in search of a decent bowl of gumbo. However, he currently resides in the Prospect Heights neighborhood of Brooklyn with his wife and dog Thor. He's a frequent speaker at industry conferences, including Software Development, Dr. Dobb's Architecure & Design World, SD Best Practices, Extreme Markup Languages, and too many user groups to count. His open source projects include the XOM Library for processing XML with Java and the Amateur media player.

Colophon

The animal on the cover of *JavaMail API* is a little pied cormorant.

The cover image's origin is unknown. The cover font is Adobe ITC Garamond. The text font is Adobe Minion Pro; the heading font is Adobe Myriad Condensed; and the code font is Dalton Maag's Ubuntu Mono.

Have it your way.

Get even more for your money.

Join the O'Reilly Community, and register the O'Reilly books you own. It's free, and you'll get:

- $4.99 ebook upgrade offer
- 40% upgrade offer on O'Reilly print books
- Membership discounts on books and events
- Free lifetime updates to ebooks and videos
- Multiple ebook formats, DRM FREE
- Participation in the O'Reilly community
- Newsletters
- Account management
- 100% Satisfaction Guarantee

Signing up is easy:

1. Go to: oreilly.com/go/register
2. Create an O'Reilly login.
3. Provide your address.
4. Register your books.

Note: English-language books only

To order books online:

oreilly.com/store

For questions about products or an order:

orders@oreilly.com

To sign up to get topic-specific email announcements and/or news about upcoming books, conferences, special offers, and new technologies:

elists@oreilly.com

For technical questions about book content:

booktech@oreilly.com

To submit new book proposals to our editors:

proposals@oreilly.com

O'Reilly books are available in multiple DRM-free ebook formats. For more information:

oreilly.com/ebooks

Spreading the knowledge of innovators   oreilly.com

Lightning Source UK Ltd.
Milton Keynes UK
UKHW031813060223
416559UK00010B/1868